HOWE·LIBRARY

HANOVER
NEW HAMPSHIRE

THE TOWN GARDENER'S COMPANION

The TOWN GARDENER'S *Companion*

FELICITY BRYAN

Illustrated by Sheilagh Noble

ANDRE DEUTSCH

For Simon

First published 1981 by
André Deutsch Limited
105 Great Russell Street London WC1

Copyright © 1981 by Felicity Bryan
All rights reserved
Phototypeset by MS Filmsetting Ltd, Frome, Somerset
Printed in Great Britain by
Ebenezer Baylis and Son Limited
The Trinity Press, Worcester and London

ISBN 0 233 97351 6

C✓

CONTENTS

List of Colour Plates *vi*
Acknowledgements *vii*
Introduction *ix*

MARCH *1*

The pleasure of herbs. Early spring flowers. Prune your roses. Decorative vegetables. Tomatoes. Rock gardens. Chrysanthemums and dahlias. Herbaceous plants.

APRIL *15*

Blossom and bulbs. Spring vegetable sowing. Unusual vegetables. Camellias. Tools for summer. Your new lawn. Timeless annuals. Grow some wine.

MAY *29*

The May Gap. Growing azaleas. Greenhouses. Gro-bags. The chemistry of gardening. The outdoor room. Summer bedding. Window boxes. Shady plants.

JUNE *43*

Peonies. Urban farming. Office vegetables. Hang up your plants. New York interlude. Miniature roses. The friendly weed. Pests. Plants for dry weather.

JULY *59*

Garden visiting. Yellow gardens. Roses old and new. White gardens. Ground cover. Thyme lawns. Shrub cuttings. Propagate geraniums. Sowing winter vegetables.

AUGUST *75*

The constant rose. Cultivating neighbours. Strawberries. *Fraises des bois*. Flowers indoors. Tips on arranging flowers. Drying for winter. Saving seeds. Roof gardens in town.

SEPTEMBER *91*

Designing a garden. Bulbs indoors. Violas. Sweet peas. Variegated shrubs. Basements.

OCTOBER *105*

Autumn glow. Planting fruit. Hard fruit. Planting for spring. Spring bulbs. Digging in compost and manure.

NOVEMBER *117*

Tree gazing. Tree planting. Evergreen trees. Choosing a tree. Silver trees. Winter window boxes. Tender plants. The romance of lilac. Making compost.

DECEMBER *129*

Picking seeds. The glory of lilies. Holly and ivy. Christmas decor. Save Christmas plants. Grow heathers. Grow pips.

JANUARY *143*

Winter colours. Time to spray. Bulbs for summer. Test your seeds. Easy house-plants. Heavenly clematis.

FEBRUARY *157*

Seed sowing. Reflective pools. Potatoes. Tactful climbers. Feed your soil. Hebes.

APPENDICES *171*
INDEX *179*

COLOUR PLATES

PLATE 1 Some town gardens   *between pages 38 and 39*
PLATE 2 Spring favourites
Tulipa tarda, Anemone blanda, Helleborus orientalis, Euphorbia epithymoides, Euphorbia characias, Iris stylosa
PLATE 3 Summer Favourites
Hemerocallis, Verbascum, *Hosta crispula, Alchemilla mollis, Lilium auratum*, Agapanthus
PLATE 4 Roses
Felicité et Perpetué, Fantin Latour, Pink Grootendorst, Ballerina, Iceberg, Lilli Marlene
PLATE 5 Shrubs   *between pages 102 and 103*
Hebe andersonii, Philadelphus coronarius aurea, Choisya ternata, Camellia Donation, *Mahonia* Charity, *Elaeagnus pungens* Aureovariegata
PLATE 6 Felicity's Garden Before
PLATE 7 Felicity's Garden After
PLATE 8 Climbers
Rose, Mme Grégoire Staechelin; Rose, New Dawn; Ceanothus, Gloire de Versailles; *Humulus lupulus aureus; Clematis orientalis;* Rose, Mermaid

Photographs by The Harry Smith Horticultural Photographic Collection, John Brookes and the author.

Acknowledgements

The Town Gardener's Companion includes many of the thoughts and schemes I had while working as gardening correspondent of London's *Evening Standard*. I would like to thank Trevor Grove who as Features Editor first risked employing me and Dick Garret who continued the good work of supplying the encouragement and kindness a feature writer needs. I wish to thank the former editor Charles Wintour for permitting me to use extracts from pieces published in the paper. Thanks also to David Harsent, my editor at André Deutsch, for suggesting that I write the book and to his cheerful and thoughtful assistant, Ariane Goodman. Sheilagh Noble's illustrations are to me total magic. I could not have wished for others. Nothing would have been written without the help of Beryl Drinkwater who appeared cheerfully at midday every Saturday over four months acting as typist/encourager/deadline. Alasdair Clayre gave me a rooftop garden to transform and boundless encouragement. During my years on the *Standard* many, many people have written giving ideas and asking advice which has always been helpful. Gardening writers are a friendly, generous breed and many gave me tips, especially Clay Jones of Dobies who could be 'phoned for advice whatever the hour. My deep thanks also go to Cob Stenham who, by giving me the run of his half acre in Highgate, allowed my ideas full rein. I would like to thank Daniel O'Conner with whom I have dug and planted over the years. Finally, it was Simon Jenkins, to whom this book is dedicated, who first put to me the bizarre suggestion that I turn my pen to gardening, thus opening up a whole new world to me. To him my debt cannot be expressed.

Introduction

THIS BOOK is addressed principally to town gardeners – that burgeoning and plucky breed so ignored in much gardening literature. That does not mean that much of it may not be entirely appropriate to people gardening in country cottages. But the emphasis is on the challenges faced by people in urban and suburban areas who tend to be short on space but not enthusiasm and who want to make the very most of what area they have. They suffer the dilemmas of finding a happy compromise between privacy and light; of tending gardens, parts of which hardly see the sun; of trying to feed the family on a small patch; of gardening with plants entirely housed in tubs; of having only a damp basement or windy roof extension in which to express those imaginations longing to be let loose. I hope, if nothing else, to help keep up their enthusiasm – for, as a town gardener myself, my own is pretty unquenchable.

Much of what I have written is based on the four years I spent as the gardening correspondent of London's *Evening Standard*. No city in the world can contain as many keen gardeners as London. A revered gardening expert once suggested that I must find it 'restricting' writing for London readers; after all, they had so little space. Restricting? I could hardly believe my ears. Challenging, more like. Did this doyen of the trade not realize just how much food could be grown in a tub or what potential a north-facing small roof garden could provide? Did he not know that Highgate allotments had one of the most beautiful views in the country or that in parts of Ealing and Hampstead you could find cottage gardens as enchanting and countrified as those in deepest Suffolk? I know many gardeners who by careful choice of plants get as much pleasure and interest from forty feet by twenty feet of land as they would from an acre.

Over the four years I wrote the column, I tended a large roof garden with over fifty tubs to water; did a stint with an allotment; moved to a traditional long, thin London back garden crammed to bursting with herbs, flowers and shrubs; and did much replanting in a glorious acre of garden in Highgate. Then I moved house and a new challenge loomed. Few country dwellers would know such variety. My years as a gardening writer had been a journey of discovery. Before I started the column I really gardened on my own, occasionally exchanging seeds with the Greeks over the fence and boring my non-gardening friends with my triumphs and discoveries. Once I began putting my schemes into print I found myself one of a huge club. It has neither rules nor subscription but the members are joined by that strongest of bonds, a love of gardening, together with a pleasantly smug feeling that they share a secret pleasure non-gardeners cannot comprehend.

Nobody wants to read a whole book to find out what they should be doing at a given time, so at the beginning of every month is a calendar giving the basics. Then, at the end, I've added several appendices giving useful addresses, books and lists of plants suitable for shady spots, for growing in tubs and for ground cover.

Nobody gardens in a town without learning to look on the bright side of things: by and large we suffer less from weeds than country dwellers who get them flying in from the surrounding fields. Our gardens are generally warmer because they are more sheltered and surrounded by heated buildings. While this book is based largely on London experience it is appropriate to other towns. In the farthest north think about two weeks later. In matters of timing, however, a gardener must, when it comes to the crunch, learn to think with his nose. If you go slavishly by any book things can go wrong. For every area is that bit different from another in soil and temperature and every February is that bit different from the last. Consult your gardening neighbours for their experience and learn from your own. And I wish you happy gardening.

MARCH

FLOWERS AND SHRUBS

❧Prune your roses any fine day, and give them rose fertilizer. ❧If the weather is good start growing seeds of hardy annuals like sweet peas, cornflowers etc. outside. ❧Prune back hardy shrubs notably buddleia and *Hydrangea paniculata*. ❧Cut fuchsias down to near ground level. ❧Plant out herbaceous plants either bought or sown from seed last summer. ❧Heathers can be planted from now for the next 2 months. ❧Plant summer bulbs of lilies and nerines and also corms of gladioli. ❧Take dahlia and chrysanthemum cuttings or divide up tubers and clumps for May planting. ❧Plant out alpines ordered from nurseries.

VEGETABLES, FRUIT AND HERBS

❧Sow broad beans early in the month. ❧In fine weather sow seeds of cabbage, peas, lettuce, carrots, cauliflower, celery, onions, parsnips, radishes, spinach, turnips and shallots. Plant leeks and brussels in seed bed. French beans can be sown under glass. ❧Plant out early potatoes towards the end of the month if fine – otherwise wait. ❧Finish planting currant and raspberry bushes and mulch them. ❧Plant out herb plants. Sow herb seeds outdoors in late March.

PLANTS UNDER PROTECTION

❧Sow a new lot of sweet peas, and continue the sowing started last month. Annuals should be either in propagators on the window sill or in seed trays in a heated greenhouse. ❧Start feeding your overwintered geraniums with liquid fertilizer. Prick out large seedlings planted last month and pot into larger trays or individual pots. ❧Sow tomatoes, peppers, cucumbers and courgettes under glass.

LAWNS

❧Reseed areas that are patchy. ❧Cut the grass on a fine day when it is about 2 in. high. Aerate the lawn. ❧Sow new lawns which have been well prepared last autumn and in the previous month.

FOR ME the gardening year begins in March and so it seems appropriate to begin this book there. True, a lot of the bolder little bulbs and early flowering shrubs are already out. But it is only now that I feel the sap rising in my own veins and, as the evenings get lighter, long to be home from work in time to prune those roses which have suddenly made a burst or to give the lawn its first mow of the year. A few sunny days this month will make your garden move before your very eyes as plants you had forgotten having planted way back in the autumn cheekily surprise you with their young shoots. Suddenly there are a hundred and ten jobs to be done.

The pleasure of herbs

Every spring, along with the many routine chores, a gardener needs a new venture; something which will make the garden just a bit special this year, whether it be a new pergola or a rearrangement of the vegetable garden. One spring, my project was a herb garden. I cut off the last ten feet at the bottom of my long thin lawn, laid a square pattern of old bricks, divided the area up into tiny beds and placed a stone Chinese goddess from a junk shop (not a common sight in Holloway back yards) serenely in the middle.

She gave it a centre. Around her feet, come summer, would spring the bushes of blue flowered hyssop and clumps of chives and larger clumps like fennel and lovage. Around the edge of the square I planted lavender to form a low silvery hedge and in the four corners I placed attractive pots containing mint (which should not be let loose in a flower bed or it will take over). There are many varieties of mint, from the common spearmint, which is a must with new potatoes, to apple mint, pineapple mint and the beautiful soft yellow variegated mint which looks so fetching. You can put those tender herbs like basil into pots also: it is a wonderful addition to summer salads but is a herb which needs a lot of warmth and sun to keep it going. Basil also comes in a deep beetroot-coloured variety.

Most of the herbs in such a garden will be used for cooking. Remember that thyme comes in silver and variegated golden colours in addition to the common thyme. Rosemary bushes will grow quite tall so should be placed at the back. Savory is a lovely summer addition and I would never be without clumps of sorrel which, though not especially attractive, is so useful to add to salads and makes a wonderful soup itself. Sage also comes in a soft yellow variegated form and a reddish one as well as the normal grey-green. It grows in attractive clumps. Golden marjoram is delicious in tomato salads and spreads prettily.

Herbs have a romance and lore all of their own. They have played an essential part in people's lives since the ancient Greeks. Every Elizabethan household required a well-stocked herb garden, many of whose formal layouts survive. A glance at *Culpeper's Complete Herbal* (early seventeenth century) shows the multifarious uses of herbs as well as the suspicion and myth attached to them. Though Culpeper concentrated on their healing powers – basil for expelling afterbirth, marjoram for curing toothache – they can pep up our bland processed foods just as they disguised ill-preserved meat then.

You should grow non-edible herbs like lavender, lovely fluffy cotton lavender (santolina) and enchanting blue rue for their fine silvery looks and amazing smells. What's more they are evergreen – in fact ever*silver* – so will give the garden a fine shape in winter. If you have only a tiny garden you could do a lot worse than put the whole thing over to herbs, intricately plotted.

Many herbs can be sown from seed – under glass now or in the open in April. Some seed companies put out a special herb selection. Things like chives, savory, tarragon, marjoram, fennel, parsley, thyme and sorrel will come up easily this way. Others like rosemary or sage are better taken from cuttings in summer. Herbs fetch a good price and you might set up a trade with the local health food shop. If you want to buy existing plants and have a wider choice you might write off now to one of the many herb nurseries which have sprung up in recent years (see Appendix VI). Finally, for your centre-piece you might replace my goddess with a lovely slow-growing (though horribly expensive) bay-tree.

Early spring flowers

The secret about placing early-flowering plants is to site them near the house where you can appreciate them without having to trundle down to the bottom of the garden in a March gale. Not nearly enough people plant early flowers in their front gardens; they put a spring in your step every morning as you leave for work and provide equal pleasure to passers by. So it is worth doing a 'recce' now – as suddenly the snowdrops are joined by primroses and crocuses and the tiny cyclamineus narcissi, a bare three inches tall, bob their brilliant yellow heads beside the purple and blue *Iris reticulata* – to see how you could plan to cheer up your own garden next March. . . . Make notes; for come autumn planting time you will have forgotten.

A visit to your local park is a start, but by now many of the other gardens are opening to inspire you and you might also spy on your neighbours. Few gardeners do not enjoy telling you about the plants that are their pride. By a friend's entrance door at present grows the soft mauve *Iris unguicularis*, so beautiful with its delicate yellow markings that it takes your breath away. This Algerian iris, which grows to about a foot, flowers throughout the winter and just now has become my favourite flower.

Other surprises are the early bergenias. These are those rather maligned plants often called elephants' ears on account of their large, flat, glossy leaves. But they are useful, being evergreen and not minding shade; and in early spring they produce interesting, hyacinth-like flowers. *Bergenia schmidtii* is a particularly lovely soft pink flower much loved of the famous gardening writer Gertrude Jekyll.

Another family of flowers whose winter beauty makes me weak at the knees are hellebores. The best known is the Christmas rose, *Helleborus niger* which is so welcome in December. But more spectacular are the *H. orientalis*, which come in a variety of colours from a luminous white, through soft green to plum. What I particularly love are the inner markings of the flowers which are generally beautifully spotted in crimson and maroon. Most hellebores have magnificent evergreen foliage, grow happily in most soil and actually prefer a little shade.

My favourite hellebore, and quite the oddest, is *H. corsicus*. It is a bushy plant with the most striking leaves of all that possess a positively sculpted appearance with their sharp edges of deep, glossy green. The flowers themselves open in quantities of the softest, luminous green bell shapes on stalks about two feet tall. They can look particularly spectacular when juxtaposed with other flowers, an obvious example being early blue *Iris reticulata* – the effect is electric. In one garden at Kew there is a whole flowerbed devoted to them which makes a visit worthwhile at any time from February through to April.

There is no doubt that green flowers hold for me a special fascination and I am therefore drawn to euphorbias very much in the same way I am to hellebores. About now *Euphorbia characias* makes a dramatic entry – all three feet of her. Euphorbias are all relatives of our native wood spurge with its primitive-looking green flowers. In truth what you see are not flowers but bracts which surround the very insignificant tiny flowers. The plants grow in striking clumps and have dark evergreen leaves which look fine in winter. But just now the bracts are putting on a quite breathtaking display.

Prune your roses

To prune or not to prune? It's a question that vexes some otherwise quite competent gardeners as many a leggy, sprawling rose bush bears witness. In fact rose pruning is a quite simple and – weather permitting – restful occupation which you should have got behind you before this month is through.

The vast majority of bush roses in English gardens are hybrid teas and floribundas. If I had my way there would be a more judicious mix of old-fashioned musks and hybrid perpetuals which flower less but are more delicate and ravishing in their individual flowers. But the fact remains that most of us British like red roses best followed by orange and yellow, with the pinks and whites bringing up the rear; and above all we like perpetual flowering hybrid teas and floribundas which are comparative newcomers.

The first floribunda was developed in 1924 and hybrid teas are about 100 years old. Their blooms appear on vigorous new growth made in the spring. It stands to reason that if you don't cut back some of last year's growth, a rose that continues doing this will be all leg, a haphazard shape, and have little energy to produce flowers. So pruning is investing in the future by cutting back last year's growth. Most people do this by about half. Wherever you cut, the rule is that it should always be just above a bud – say a quarter of an inch – and at an angle of forty-five degrees parallel to the angle the bud is facing. Don't cut higher above the bud or that bit of stem will die off. Cut sharply and neatly. As the bud will grow into a stem, cut above one that is facing outwards so that the bush makes a good shape rather than growing inwards to become a tangled mess.

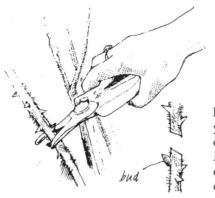

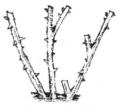

Rose pruning. Reduce the size of your bush by about half, cutting out dead wood and weak shoots. Make the cut just above an outward-facing bud so that the line of the cut is parallel to the bud.

Hard pruning – which is cutting the bush down to just a few buds above the ground – should only be done with newly planted roses. Medium pruning, which is what I do, removes all dead wood and spindly growth, then cuts the bush down to about half size, leaving a few firm stems to form the basis for next year's growth.

Climbers – which are really just bush roses which are trained to climb – should not be pruned from the top or they will give up climbing altogether and revert to a bush. However, cut out dead wood, flimsy side growth and last year's hips. Then cut the side shoots from the main stems back by about half. Standard roses should be firmly cut back to about four to six buds. With ramblers it's too late; you should prune them hard back to their base in October as they flower on the new stems growing now.

When you have done your pruning, burn the prunings if you can. They have no place on the compost heap where they become brittle and spikey. And talking of spikes, no sane gardener should ever embark on her pruning without being well equipped with tough gloves. I speak as an insane one who annually tears her hands disgracefully.

Roses survive most conditions wonderfully but definitely flower better if well fed. So when the pruning is over rake some general fertilizer or a special rose fertilizer into the soil. Repeat this again as the buds begin to form and they will be off to a good start. I always put a good load of manure on my roses in the autumn.

If you visit specialist rose gardens like those of the Royal National

Rose Society at St Albans and the rose gardens in Regents Park you will notice that the beds contain only roses. I think that this is a mistake in a garden. Granted, the roses may flower that little bit better if left alone. But the rose bed looks really bereft and dead throughout the winter and I think the great joy of roses is mixing them up with other things.

So about now get planning and planting other things in your rose beds. I had a great friend who mixed fuchsias with them a lot. But like roses, fuchsias are not evergreen. I find that lavender, and other silver-leaved plants and shrubs like *Senecio greyi* and the many varieties of feathery silver artemisia, provide a wonderful backing to roses. Then at the back of your rose bed put evergreen shrubs like *Viburnum tinus* and the various kinds of mahonia (Charity, which flowers with lemon-yellow scented racemes in January is my favourite) which will provide winter colour and then give a dense backdrop to your bright roses in summer, enhancing them all the more.

Decorative vegetables

As you continue your seed sowing programme started under glass in February, give a thought to the look of your vegetables. In the summer of the drought a friend invited me to see her small garden in Islington. As I entered the patch (about sixteen feet square) which she was studiously watering with her bath water, I saw a blaze of colours. It took a few seconds to realize that this gay garden was entirely planted in vegetables. Different coloured leaves juxtaposed, light green by dark purple by yellow, looked wonderfully bold arranged, not in rows, but in clumps and shapes. Up the fence grew white- and red-flowered beans and then, of course, there were the tomatoes and the flowering herbs.

So if your garden is tiny but you wish to use it to grow pretty vegetables here are a few suggestions. Climbing runner beans with their pillar-box red flowers were introduced to Britain in 1633 as ornamental plants. In Denmark I have seen them grown indoors for decoration. So grow them up your fence, contrasting them with a white-flowered runner bean like Fry and the pale pink Sunset. Globe artichokes have magnificent silver foliage but do need lots of width and height to grow to three to four feet. A small clump could make a fine corner feature and give delicious artichokes in the second and third year if well fed. Nearer the ground, custard marrows or golden zucchini, with their yellow flowers and fruit, look bold and gay.

I am no kale eater, but many of the decorative kales and chards are edible. Beetroot, of course, has fine deep wine foliage. More useful are lettuces. These should be grown in succession starting them off in seed boxes and then planting out as young plants about two inches high – though if you do this after August they will bolt. Two particularly pretty varieties are Continuity, which is an unusual reddish colour and Salad Bowl, which is a non-hearting lettuce with many lime-green curly leaves. Peppers are especially attractive bushes when green, and when the peppers themselves turn red they look very splendid indeed. So, of course, do tomatoes.

A riot of tomatoes

Out of the goodness of his heart a friend once returned from a trip to Italy laden not with Chianti but with exotic Italian seeds. Packets displayed wild-looking lettuces, eight kinds of varied coloured chicory and – best of all – a lugubrious-faced tomato called San Marzano. Instructions on the back told me in five languages (would that our seed merchants were so cosmopolitan) that I should grow this tomato very much as I normally do in my greenhouse – and it was a success. Why is it that many quite proficient gardeners still grow Moneymaker year by year when ringing the changes can be such fun?

If, like me, you grow four different kinds of tomato each year, you will end up comparing flavours with the concentration of a wine taster. At one Chelsea Flower Show, Fisons – to promote their excellent gro-bags – put on a display of around forty different tomato varieties. The snag of course is that if you buy plants many nurseries give you little choice. So if you wish to be bold, and also save considerable expense, you should grow them from seed starting in a seed tray or pots under glass this month. You might grow one kind and swap it with your neighbour's growth.

So with due respect to Moneymaker here are a few suggestions. There are two kinds of tomato: the standard kind grown by professionals and many ordinary gardeners which need stakes and whose side shoots must be rigorously removed so they do not spread (I have seen tomato plants growing to thirty feet long and trained along vine supports in commercial greenhouses in Guernsey). The second is the bush variety which generally produces smaller fruit over a longer period and is much easier to tend. Nearly all are happy if kept outdoors. Wherever they grow they need a lot of sun to ripen.

The bush variety of tomatoes I love is Pixie, with smallish, very tasty fruit. Sleaford Abundance has been popular for many years and you should also try The Amateur, Sigmabush and French Cross. Tiny Tim and Sub-Arctic Cherry have delicious cherry-sized fruit to put whole in salads. They are also fun in pots indoors. Of the standard varieties Ware Cross and Alicante have quite especially good flavours, I think. Ailsa Craig is very popular and I always grow sweet Carter's Fruit. Yellow tomatoes not only look pretty but taste sweet and rather plummy. Try Yellow Plum, Yellow Perfection or Golden Sunrise. If you are even more daring you could try the continental ones. Marmande is a firm friend with large bulbous fruit. Tigrella has gay stripey red and yellow fruit which arrives quite early. Of the long varieties Roma is easy to find and produces a good crop. It is the sort Italians use for ketchup and spaghetti sauces. It has few pips and so is strongly recommended for making tasty tomato soups.

Gardening with rocks

I have a private theory that half the rock gardens in towns begin life as builders' rubble. No less than three builders in my time have said to me when faced with a pile of rubble: 'Well, you could get a skip. But that's expensive and you'll need a permit. So why not just cover it over and make a nice rock garden?' I have always gone the skip route for there is nothing more selfish to your successors – and annoying to yourself if you change your plans – than leaving builders' rubble in a garden. I also think that an isolated, rather surprised-looking rock garden in an urban setting does not always come off. However, you can use enchanting rock plants in many other settings and now is a good time to plant.

If money and space were no object, I would invest much time and some trouble in a rock garden on the lines of the glorious one at the Royal Horticultural Society's gardens at Wisley, which covers a whole sunny hillside. As few gardeners have space for more than a token rockery it is worth pondering other uses for alpines, which include in their number some of the brightest-eyed, most beautiful flowers in creation.

In May and June my tubs are a riot of mauves, pinks, whites and yellows as the aubrietias, saxifrage, arabis and alyssum – those stalwarts of every country cottage dry stone wall – burst into flower. Later come the campanulas and small geraniums, all of them traditionally rock plants but plainly at home in my most un-alpine of settings, blooming alongside the annuals. You may wish to be more purist and set aside a special area like an old stone sink, a large tub or a raised bed exclusively for rock plants. Whatever you do they are ideal for small spaces. Will Ingwersen, a well-known rock plant specialist and proprietor of one of the best rock plant nurseries in the world, reckons that when using tiny plants you can fit about fifty different alpines into a trough measuring two feet by three feet.

Bear in mind that most of the alpines which you will plant in the next month or so come from high, mountainous spots where the sun is bright, rainfall is plentiful and drainage is very good. So few rock plants will flourish in a damp and shady basement or under trees or against a north wall. Put a good layer of crocks in a trough or shallow tub followed by a layer of lumpy compost material which will guarantee them good drainage. Then fill it with a balanced loamy soil, mixing in some bonemeal to give the plants a good start.

When choosing your plants always consider their eventual size. Aubrietias or campanulas will soon swamp a miniature garden. So select small, clumpy species like enchanting pink *Androsace carnea* or soft pink *Armeria caespitosa*. Gentians are a must as are little tufts of pinks like *Dianthus alpinus*. Certain succulent rock plants are resistent to drought and therefore just right for shallow tubs. These include sedums which come in an enormous variety of colours and sizes. They are easy to propagate by dividing them about now. I love *S.* Ruby Glow which has deep red flowers in late summer – and lots of them, lasting a good long time.

There is such a huge choice of rock plants that it is worth writing up for one of the catalogues (see Appendix VI) to get a full selection. But a few other suggestions are baby potentillas which will flower over a long period in the summer with delightful single open flowers. I am dotty about rock roses (helianthemum) which again flower in summer in clumps of very delicate single flowers which can be numbered in their hundreds. The different varieties range from white, through yellow and orange to subtle pinks and deep crimson. They should be cut back after flowering as they get straggly otherwise. You can propagate from cuttings now. Little blue veronicas are another favourite; they flower in mid-summer, lasting for several months.

Of course buying individual plants can be expensive. But many of these can be grown from seed if you get your skates on and sow them under glass during this month. Most seed companies sell rock garden selections. Saxifrage, alyssum, aubrietia, dianthus, iberis, edelweiss, helianthemum, campanulas, arabis and gentians should all be quite easy to grow and are so satisfying. Just now of course the little rock garden bulbs are ravishing. But I shall deal with them in the autumn which is the time to plant them.

Chrysanthemums and dahlias

In wet periods this month, when all you want to do is stay indoors, you can quell your frustration by planning for May when – once the frosts are truly gone – you can plant out those flowers of late summer and autumn warmth: the bold chrysanthemums and dahlias.

I have always loved chrysanthemums and it was a great honour for me when Mrs Hall, who runs a chrysanthemum nursery, named one of her new creations – a very pretty mauve-pink described in the catalogue as 'weatherproof' and 'offered after extensive trial' – after me. . . . About dahlias, however, I have mixed feelings as so many of them are bred to look as if made of shocking pink or red plastic with a candy-stripe added for good measure. Like chrysanthemums, they come in all sizes from the whoppers with huge heads rising to five feet at the back of the border (a friend of mine once described one exhibit of magnum chrysanthemums at a show as looking like a display of swimming caps) to the compact little sprays of Dandy which grows twenty inches tall. Whatever shape or colour, dahlias and chrysanthemums have the glorious advantage of flowering continually from July until the first frosts – before which you should bring them in to the protection of a shed or frame.

Chrysanthemums are hardy perennials, but it is advisable to overwinter them under cover. Dahlias are half hardy which means that tubers must be dug up and overwintered away from frost. But given this modicum of attention they are the best possible investment and can increase from year to year. To increase your stock, dahlia tubers and chrysanthemum clumps should be divided now. But an even better way to propagate is by taking cuttings this month.

If your plants are potted up they should be producing many little shoots which, once they become about three inches long, are ready for cutting. From one plant you can raise at least ten smaller ones for flowering this year. As with all cuttings you need a good sterilized peat or cutting compost with a handful of silver sand (the experts tend to advise half peat and half sand) mixed in for the tiny roots to cling to. A propagator is the perfect container for cuttings. But pots will also be fine.

Cut off your three-inch shoots, remove the bottom couple of leaves so that you have a neat stalk to plant in the compost. Firm this in about an inch deep. When all are in position, water the cuttings with a fine spray. Keep them away from direct sunlight and in two to three weeks they should be standing up perkily and making it on their own. At this point plant them in pots or in a bigger tray full of good compost like John Innes No 1. Once planted, the cuttings should be kept in a light place where there is no chance of them getting frosted or drying out. The temperature should be around 50°F, and they should be kept moist but not wet.

Herbaceous plants

According to old gardeners' lore the wise gardener plants out his herbaceous border in the autumn. At this time, the saying goes, the ground is still warm, your plants will have a good start and the weather is less temperamental. Only mugs like myself wait until March when the ground is cold and waterlogged and the rain – or snow – begins each time you put on your wellingtons. However, after a really cold winter we fools can feel quite smug when many of the tenderer plants have fallen victim to long periods of being frozen stiff in their first year out. Nowadays it seems that many of the nurseries agree with me, since they send out their plants by post around this time. Also now the garden centres are awash with delphiniums and other plants from which to choose.

Technically, herbaceous plants – more correctly called hardy perennials – will live for more than two years. They will increase and multiply and will prove a marvellous investment, provided they are given some attention by being divided up once they get too thick after, say, three years and also by being fed regularly with manure or compost in the autumn and general fertilizer in the spring. Such old favourites as lupins, delphiniums, hostas, day lilies, peonies (though peonies should not be divided but left undisturbed for many years), Michaelmas daisies, pinks, phlox and aquilegia, to name but a few, come into this category.

Of course few of us in built-up areas have space or time for the old-fashioned herbaceous border – a good ten feet deep by forty feet long – for which English gardens are so famed. Besides, herbaceous plants die back in winter which is a sorry sight from one's kitchen window. The answer is a mixed border, i.e. a collection of shrubs and hardy perennials planted so that evergreen shrubs like hebe and choisya can lighten the gloom in winter and then, come summer, provide an attractive background when the prima donnas like the peonies make their entrance. In and among these, plant some summer bulbs like lilies, glorious pale rose *Amaryllis belladonna* and deep pink *Nerine bowdenii*, which should go on from year to year. Remember to label bulbs or you will forget where you planted them and an enthusiastic dig might well carve a lily bulb in two.

As the young plants get going, during the first and second years, there are bound to be gaps unless you have heavily overplanted. So fill these in, when June arrives, with annuals like larkspur, tobacco plants, love-in-a-mist and cornflowers. I think it is important to make a plan. Ideally you will have done this in the winter months when ordering your plants from a catalogue while sitting and dreaming by the fire. When it comes to planning I find the RHS handbook *Herbaceous Plants* very helpful as you need always to know the height and flowering time and colour if the glorious painting that you have in your head is going to take place before your eyes. Miss Jekyll took to gardening when her eyesight failed and she was no longer able to paint. The laying of a herbaceous garden is the nearest I ever get to painting and every bit as exciting.

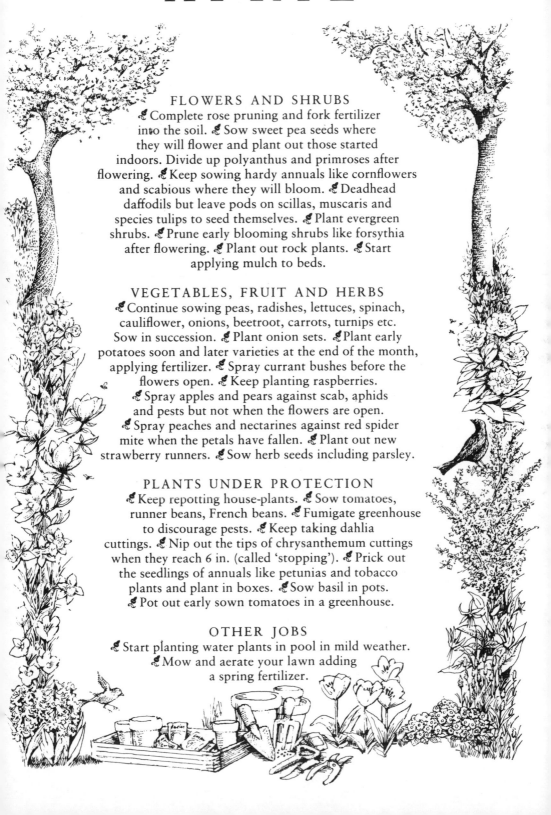

APRIL

FLOWERS AND SHRUBS
Complete rose pruning and fork fertilizer
into the soil. Sow sweet pea seeds where
they will flower and plant out those started
indoors. Divide up polyanthus and primroses after
flowering. Keep sowing hardy annuals like cornflowers
and scabious where they will bloom. Deadhead
daffodils but leave pods on scillas, muscaris and
species tulips to seed themselves. Plant evergreen
shrubs. Prune early blooming shrubs like forsythia
after flowering. Plant out rock plants. Start
applying mulch to beds.

VEGETABLES, FRUIT AND HERBS
Continue sowing peas, radishes, lettuces, spinach,
cauliflower, onions, beetroot, carrots, turnips etc.
Sow in succession. Plant onion sets. Plant early
potatoes soon and later varieties at the end of the month,
applying fertilizer. Spray currant bushes before the
flowers open. Keep planting raspberries.
Spray apples and pears against scab, aphids
and pests but not when the flowers are open.
Spray peaches and nectarines against red spider
mite when the petals have fallen. Plant out new
strawberry runners. Sow herb seeds including parsley.

PLANTS UNDER PROTECTION
Keep repotting house-plants. Sow tomatoes,
runner beans, French beans. Fumigate greenhouse
to discourage pests. Keep taking dahlia
cuttings. Nip out the tips of chrysanthemum cuttings
when they reach 6 in. (called 'stopping'). Prick out
the seedlings of annuals like petunias and tobacco
plants and plant in boxes. Sow basil in pots.
Pot out early sown tomatoes in a greenhouse.

OTHER JOBS
Start planting water plants in pool in mild weather.
Mow and aerate your lawn adding
a spring fertilizer.

Blossom and bulbs

THAT IS WHAT April means to me as by the middle of the month my old pear tree takes on the look of a bridal hat, joining the riot of blossom of the almonds and ornamental cherries in the neighbouring gardens. This is the time when residential areas with front gardens look their loveliest, showing so much of their beauty to the passer by. The brilliant yellow forsythia which springs up everywhere looks cheerful on the drabbest day. If you have no room for a potentially large flowering tree, even a small garden will have space for the charming erect Japanese cherry called Ama no Gawa. I used to grow one in a tub in a roof garden and it gave me two weeks of total joy when its light pink blossoms appeared in April.

If you are thinking of planting a flowering tree next autumn, do your research now when most of them are in full display. A trip to a garden like Kew where they are all conveniently labelled makes the job that much easier – but most gardeners would be happy to tell you about their own. If you have the space, a weeping cherry in your front lawn can take your breath away. A specially lovely one is *Prunus* Cheal's Weeping. Just now its long branches which sweep right to the ground are covered in bright pink double flowers. Another charming weeper is *P. subhirtella* Pendula Rubra with its deep rose single flowers.

I always prefer the white and soft-pink flowers to the rather more garish, though extremely popular, sugar-pink double flowers of Kanzan. *Prunus* is a confusing name for though it literally means plum it covers the ornamental varieties of almond, cherry, peach and plum, none of which should be planted in the hope of good edible fruit come autumn. Another lovely and unusual cherry is the *P. padus* Grandiflora which has long racemes of white flowers towards the end of the month. To get a good idea of the scope of this amazing genus (for there are literally hundreds of varieties of *Prunus*) write up for a good catalogue (see Appendix VI).

It may seem odd to talk of next spring when all summer lies ahead. But as you look round at intoxicating gardens (and by the end of this month many larger gardens are opening to the public) it is worth doing a post mortem on your own small patch. Does it look as lively and pretty as it could just now? Could that dreary north wall not be cheered by a breathtaking *Chaenomeles speciosa* – the lovely flowering quince which blooms now in a variety of pretty colours from soft pinky whites to the very interesting coral colours of C. *umbilicata* and the bright crimson of C. Rowallane Seedling? The C. *japonica* with its vivid orange flowers bears the best of the quinces in autumn. But all produce edible ones which are a golden yellow.

The most important things to check on now are the bulbs. Come autumn when it is time to plant you won't remember what grew where and, more important, where the gaps were. Also if you start ordering now (see Appendix VI for catalogues) you will be able to get the varieties you want instead of taking pot luck with everyone else in October. A good catalogue brims with tips on colours, shapes and sizes giving flowering times so that you can plan in succession.

It is dotty to plant only one kind of daffodil that flowers in April when the whole narcissus family is there for the asking and when, with planning, you can have different kinds flowering from January to May. It is even dottier to do as I once did and in a mean and hasty moment buy a selection from a cheap offer in the newspaper. I got what I deserved; huge dull yellow things quite out of scale with my garden. They also blew over in the gales and next year I had to give them to someone with a large orchard where they could be lost.

Smaller, more delicate narcissi are far better for tubs and naturaliz-ing in grass under your blossom trees. On a rockery or in tubs try little cyclamineus types whose petals turn back such as Jack Snape or Jumblie. They all grow about eight inches tall. Mix with jonquil types like Bobbysoxer or Demure. They seem expensive but will multiply and repay you for generations.

In my front garden and visible to the street are Ice Follies. This is a wonderfully interesting narcissus growing about sixteen inches tall. Its perianth (outer petals) is white and its short trumpet is a soft lemony yellow getting deeper at its very frilly edge. About the same height and flowering a little later comes Binkie which again is lemony yellow turning nearly white later. White daffodils are particularly striking. The best known and rightly popular is Mount Hood which you can easily get hold of. But the near-whites like Desdemona and Tibet which flower rather earlier are equally lovely and more unusual.

Of course spring is not just narcissi. There are hosts of enchanting bulbs, the ones I particularly fancy being the blue ones which look so fetching alongside the yellow and cream of narcissi or the soft yellow of primroses. If you have a grassy area where bulbs can naturalize don't fail to buy *Anemone blanda*. If left they will spread beautifully and the soft blue varieties look dazzling with daffodils. Grape hyacinths are especially striking when grouped together producing clumps of that vivid Tory blue. Finally, I have a little bank which just now is a mass of bobbing blue scillas. I can't tell you how pretty it is. They die back just as the peonies in the same spot begin to get large and I forget them until they stun me again next spring.

One of the things I always regret in April is that I failed to divide my primroses in the autumn. I can never have enough of them and they can be so easily increased by dividing them up. Of course there are a good many kinds of primroses, my favourite still being the native of our woods, the *Primula vulgaris*. But there are some other very interesting ones in soft pinks like *P. altaica*, and white and more vivid yellow ones. I never like seeing them all mixed up; a drift of one colour looks much more natural to me – perhaps contrasting happily with some nearby forget-me-nots.

Spring vegetable sowing

At the end of March and the beginning of this month spring fever gets us all and suddenly the allotments in my street are a-buzz. Easter is traditionally vegetable-sowing time, in fact old wives' lore has it that potatoes planted on Good Friday will always do best – plainly a bizarre notion when Good Fridays can be as much as four weeks apart from one year to the next, but one to which many people still superstitiously subscribe.

Assuming you spent a good few hours digging your vegetable garden in the late autumn and winter, then the frosts will have broken down your soil giving it a wonderfully crumbly feel which makes it ideal for sowing. This is called a fine tilth. First of all put on your wellington boots, for the plot will have to be well trod over to firm it before you get going with the sowing. If you have not already dug the garden over do so now to a depth of about nine inches i.e. that of a garden spade. Next, stamp it down firmly and rake the sowing area (if you work backwards you automatically tread down the soil you are to sow next as you pace up and down).

From now on a rake with a twelve-inch head is the only tool you need. It loosens up the top thin layer of soil and, when turned on its side, makes a fine V-shaped drill for your seed sowing. It has the useful extra factor of providing an accurate measure – when your seed packet says sow twenty-four inches apart, two rake heads will be the correct measure.

And so to the sowing. This should not be done hastily for it requires a degree of planning in accordance with the limited space you probably have (I make a chart every year and keep it to the next). Like any good farmer you should not sow the same crop in the same spot two years running. That way lies the possibility of disease setting in (such as club root with brassicas) and the risk, too, of poor crops if all the good that this year's vegetables require was taken by last year's crop. Green vegetables, for instance, need nitrogen. So it stands to reason that you plant them where you grew your peas and beans – which put nitrogen back into the soil – last year.

In a plot twenty feet by ten feet, which is often as much as town gardeners can afford, you have room for quite a selection of vegetables (see sketch). Divide your area up loosely into three parts. The first section is where you will grow the brassicas, by which I mean broccoli, Brussels sprouts, cabbage, cauliflower or kale. In the next section you will concentrate on root crops such as beetroot, carrots, parsnips, potatoes or swedes. In the last section come all the other vegetables such as lettuce, onions, celery, leeks, courgettes, peas and beans, radishes, tomatoes and cucumbers. Leeks, broccoli, sprouts and kale should be started in a seed bed and then planted out in their place in June by which time you will have harvested some other quick-growing vegetable in that spot already.

Next year you will ring the changes by putting the roots where the brassicas were, and so on; in this way, you find yourself growing peas (for example) in the same place only once every three years. This will give you a healthy, well-balanced soil. Of course it's never quite as organized as that and half the challenge of producing vegetables in a small space is to see how many you can fit in by following one crop on fast with the next. A very quick grower, for instance, is the radish. I tend to grow lettuces in seed trays, planting them out as young plants in succession.

When sowing your seeds, always sow in a straight line marked by a taut string. Not only will it look more orderly, but you will also know the weeds from the young vegetables when they start sprouting.

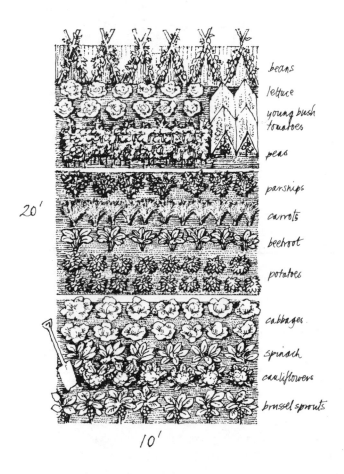

beans
lettuce
young bush tomatoes
peas
parsnips
carrots
beetroot
potatoes
cabbages
spinach
cauliflowers
brussel sprouts

20'

10'

Instructions on the packet of seeds will tell you how deep to sow in your drill and also how wide apart. Remember that the distance given on a packet assumes that you have a good-sized garden and want to grow plants of show standard. If for twelve inches you read nine, your plants will not suffer greatly. Once you have sown the seeds, rake the soil gently over them adding some fertilizer like Growmore and, if nature does not provide, give the area a light water.

Vegetables that can be sown outdoors now are potatoes, peas, broad beans, French beans, beetroot, spinach, radishes, kale, leeks, lettuce, cabbage, broccoli, onions and spring onions, parsnips, carrots, celery, cauliflower and Brussels sprouts. Later in the warmth of May or June you will plant runner beans. Tomatoes, courgettes, cucumbers and peppers should be sown under protection to be planted out again in late May if the weather looks good.

Unusual vegetables

Nowadays there are many more exotic vegetables creeping into the catalogues which offer the biggest choice, and even into the selection of packets available over the counter. Aubergine and squash (try Little Gem) are easy to grow. Sugar peas (more elegantly known as mange tout) are delicious peas of which you eat the whole pod. Chinese cabbage is marvellous in salads or cooked and should be grown like lettuce. Celeriac, which the French use a lot, is a tasty root vegetable. I tend to bring chicory seeds back from Italy or France where they have a much wider variety including many beautiful red ones. Fennel, which we grow as a herb, can be grown as a wonderful thick-stalked vegetable for salads or cooking. In a good summer you can easily grow melons in a greenhouse. Salsify is a really useful winter root vegetable which you boil and serve with butter.

Of course for gardeners with little space few things are more rewarding than lettuces. You may not realize it, but with the help of a cloche and a small plastic propagator to start them off you can extend your lettuce-growing season for six months, experimenting each year with new varieties and some old favourites. Lettuces sown under glass in February can be planted out in late March and be picked in early June. My favourite of the soft, round, butterhead varieties is Sutton's Fortune which is medium-sized with lots of heart. All The Year Round is very reliable, as its name implies. For crispheads Webb's Wonderful and Tom Thumb cannot be a better pair. Of the cos varieties Little Gem is a firm, tiny favourite with a wonderful yellow heart.

Camellias

Camellias have always held a special romance for me. Perhaps it has something to do with Garbo's role in *Camille*. Dumas's haunting story of *The Lady of the Camellias* is said to have started a run on the flowers; and still *La Traviata* draws the crowds. About now, however, it is the camellias themselves that draw us. Fans like myself make an annual pilgrimage to some especially good camellia spot like the Royal Horticultural Society's garden at Wisley. Some of the most romantic camellia gardens I know are on the edge of Lake Como and Lake Maggiore in Northern Italy. There the soil clearly suits them, as does the heavy rainfall, and they grow like trees.

There are countless varieties of these enchanting, rich, evergreen bushes with fine glossy leaves (infinitely finer than leaves of rhododendrons, alongside which camellias are often planted) and ravishing flowers. Hilliers of Winchester alone list more than 180 and they vary dramatically in character – rather like ladies at a ball: there are the blowsy, almost vulgar sugar-pink blooms of Lady Clare and the similarly showy large red-pink ones of Adolphe Audusson. Then there is the virginal white Amo-no-kawa; the many-petalled Pink Perfection, with not a petal out of place; the boisterous candy-striped Tricolor; and the gentle loveliness of warm pink Donation – to my mind the belle of the ball.

All these are hybrids of the camellias from Japan (*Camellia japonica*) which have proved hardy and ideal for our climate. In Japan they flourish in woods and so are best planted in dappled shade, getting enough sun to form buds but staying really moist. Because they bloom from March to May, the flowers are susceptible to frost and should not be planted where they will get the early morning sun which, on touching a frozen blossom, turns it brown. Industrious gardeners protect shrubs on frosty nights with sacking – but once they reach ten feet you must resort to prayer.

The snag, as with rhododendrons, is that camellias hate lime, but you can quite easily test your soil with a kit which is readily available. If it is acid you are fine. If not, and you are still determined to grow them, dig a deep hole at least two feet wide, then line the sides with polythene and fill it with peat and leafmold or a special acid compost you can buy. Use dried blood as a fertilizer and pep it up with an annual feed of Sequestrene.

My simpler solution, which is ideal for patios, balconies or basement entrances, is to plant camellias in elegant tubs. I did this with a pair of Donation in a roof garden facing north. They looked simply lovely. But with tubs it is very important to remember to keep watering, for a camellia can all too easily dry out and die.

Tools for summer

This is traditionally the time when gardeners check the contents of their tool sheds. Suddenly there is so much digging and planting to be done that you reluctantly decide that you deserve a new spade. As if by magic your trowel buckles in your hand, thus increasing the shopping list and your husband announces that after years of puffing up and down with that excellent old lawn mower he is due for an electric version.

In the 1970s there was a positive revolution in the lawnmower world. From controlling ninety per cent of the market, the mechanical push-mower has been totally outstripped by power-driven machines. There are three types: cylinder, rotary and flail (the last is not much used). Cylinder is the traditional model – the first one appeared nearly 150 years ago – and is still recommended by lawn snobs for the finest finish.

Rotary mowers are simpler and the small, cheap electric mowers like mine tend to be rotaries. Mowing with them is something akin to hoovering which might explain their popularity with women. But there are variations on the rotary, the most sophisticated being the hover mower which is supported not on wheels but on a cushion of air like a hovercraft and is excellent for rough orchards and steep slopes.

Your new lawn

In principal I'm against sexism in gardening. The unwritten law that the vegetable garden is *his* preserve and the flower beds *hers* seems completely illogical. But when it comes to lawns I have noted that men often do take them more seriously. My father, for instance, may not know an aquilegia from an alstroemeria but will regale you in some detail on the benefits of scarifying. I, conversely, have never had a good lawn, finding daisies and the occasional snowdrop a welcome – if surprising – addition.

But whether you yearn for the immaculate putting green or the more meadowy look, lawns do need a modicum of regular care. And now, just as the grass gets growing again, is time to take stock. It is also a good time to lay a new lawn.

The first debate is whether to turf or sow. Turfing is simpler, if more expensive, and it does give you an instant lawn – though remember that you must keep rolling and watering it for many months once it is laid. If you have children it may be the best answer as a lawn sown now should not be walked on, never mind played on, until the autumn. However, the problem is that you never know where the turf came from. After my last lawn was laid, I had paid up before I realized what horrible clay soil and what coarse grass had been introduced into my garden.

For a really beautiful lawn the answer is to sow. You should have dug the area over in the autumn. Dig it over again now, removing all stones and rubble. Often a new lawn is sown just after the builders have left and there is not only lots of rubble around but also much of the topsoil has been removed. If you don't have good topsoil it is worth the expense of bringing some in (ask your local garden centre for the nearest source).

But what you already have can be improved. If the soil is very heavy you can work in gritty sand at a rate of about ten pounds per square yard, using your own judgement. But if it is not heavy, then peat or rotted manure, well dug in, should do the trick.

The next – and crucial – stage is to achieve a firm, flat surface. This is done first by rolling and raking at least three times, breaking down the clods with your feet. You should then tread the soil using the time-honoured method of walking on your heels. This way you will feel any holes or uneven parts which should be filled in. When you have heeled once, rake and heel again going at right angles to your previous route. Rake once more.

Your lawn is now ready if you want to turf. If you are sowing seed you should keep raking until the tilth is very fine. Then, to get your seed off to a good start, apply a fertilizer like Growmore at a rate of about one and a half ounces per square yard a week before sowing. Seed should be sown on a dry day preferably early in the month. To ensure that you sow evenly, old hands recommend that you divide your seed supply into four and sow each portion evenly over the whole lawn, in each case walking from a different one of the four sides. Then rake the whole area.

When choosing your grass seed think first of your requirements. If it is purely ornamental you can buy one of the fine mixtures which are generally a combination of grasses called fescues and bents. If the children are going to play on it you need something that contains more ryegrass, which is tough. There is now a new ryegrass called Hunter which looks much finer than some. After sowing, your main tool will be your sprinkler. For unless the rain sees to it you must keep the new seeds regularly watered, watching out for weeds.

With an existing lawn you will probably find that after the winter it is spongy with moss. This calls for scarifying; the process by which moss and unwanted matter is pulled up. Town dwellers have not enough lawn to warrant buying a mechanical scarifyer, but a wide rake will do.

Most lawns in constant summer use get compacted and therefore would benefit from aeration. The simple process of sticking your garden fork vertically into the lawn at, say, nine-inch intervals about six inches deep should help. But you can buy a special spiker which rotates as you push it along the lawn.

To keep an established lawn smooth and well-fed good gardeners apply a spring or autumn top dressing. You can buy special lawn sand or make up your own. A recommended mixture is six parts lime-free medium sand to three parts granulated peat. The mixture should be applied dry and it is worth waiting for dry weather before embarking. The professionals use drag mats and drag bushes to even out the dressing. But on your small area the back of a rake will do, or a 'lute' – a board on a long handle.

A lawn which has heavy use will need an annual feed. Lawn fertilizers abound – generally containing a good balance of nitrogen, phosphate and potash. To avoid a patchy look, fertilizer must be evenly distributed. This is best done by hand. Divide the recommended amount into two portions. If you distribute one half walking up and down from north to south and the other going from east to west the chances are it will be quite even.

Timeless annuals

Few things can be more exciting for a child than sowing a sunflower seed and then watching it grow over the months until it towers to six feet or more. When I was little and living in the country, my mother set aside special parts of the vegetable garden where my sisters and I could have our individual plots. There of course we grew annuals, generally in straight lines but sometimes in more sophisticated patterns and clumps. So while I like the border to consist mostly of shrubs and perennials I also love filling the gaps with gay annuals like those I grew as a child. Now is the time to sow outdoors.

I always grow sweet peas. Those I have sown in the autumn will by now be quite large so the ones sown now will take over, by blooming in the later summer. Other lovely annuals are lavatera, or mallow, with its charming trumpet-like flowers (there is a very pretty soft pink one called Silver Cup). These will make fine clumps in the border. So will love-in-a-mist (nigella) which comes generally in a lovely soft blue but which also can be bought in mixed colours of pinks and whites. Cornflowers are traditionally a wonderful deep blue which is the colour I like best, but they also come in pinks and whites. The best blue of all is the scabious. The wild version is a particular treat to find on the side of a country lane with its vivid mauvy-blue, many-petalled flowers. The domestic version is larger but equally beautiful.

Try also clumps of larkspur which look like small delphiniums in lovely soft pinks, blues and whites. For all these tall annuals you will need to do a bit of staking to keep them upright. The most natural way to stake is by using dead twigs from the hedgerow or branches of beech. This also comes much less expensive than buying stakes – assuming, that is, that you can get the branches.

Other lovely border plants are godetia, viscara and of course helichrysum (straw flower), particularly if you want to dry flowers for winter. For edging try the enchanting poached egg flower (limnanthes), candytuft and calendula (the pot marigold) which children particularly love but which you should avoid if you don't like bright orange in the garden.

I am a recent convert to nasturtiums which I saw growing wild all over Madeira – the local equivalent to chickweed. They can come in a rather garish orange, but there are some lovely yellow varieties and also some deep red ones which are quite spectacular. They will grow up or cascade over anything, they don't mind a bit of drought and the leaves can even be added to a salad.

Sow all your annuals in clumps and label them immediately. Otherwise you are bound to forget and pull the seedlings up as weeds – many a family quarrel has started that way – and keep them regularly watered. They may need thinning out later in which case the spare seedlings can be transplanted to another clump.

Grow some wine

To grow a vine you do not need to live in a mediterranean climate. So why not discover what the Romans and medieval monks knew all along: vines are hardy things and most kinds can easily survive and flourish in northern climates. More and more people nowadays are planting vines both for their grapes and for their elegant looks. Sitting in the sun under an arch of vines on a fine summer day, you will happily delude yourself into imagining you are somewhere much more exotic than your own back yard.

The snag is not that the frost will kill the plants, but that they will not get enough sun or warmth for the fruit to ripen. So when planning to plant you must first choose a variety that can ripen early in cooler climates and, secondly, place your vine in the most sheltered, sunny spot you have. A south facing wall is ideal, and in southern towns, in such conditions, you could well cultivate the sort of grape recommended for greenhouse growing. As vines can produce a greater weight of fruit per square yard than any rival, you could easily grow a goodish amount to eat in a small yard, if your garden has enough sun.

And vines are delightful to look at. Those picturesque large leaves which the Greeks use for cooking turn from a light lime green in spring to a wonderful russet in autumn. A vine planted now (you can keep planting well into May) could make ten feet of growth in one year. Nor will it be fussy about soil, but obviously some compost and bonemeal worked in when planting will give it a fair start and help provide good drainage, which is a must.

A vine grown in a fourteen-inch tub could grow there for ten years, producing – once established – around eight pounds of grapes a year. So plant Chambourcin (black) and Mueller–Thurgau (German white) in large Provençal tubs against a south wall. Some other suitable outdoor varieties are Seyve Villard White, which is very vigorous; Chasselas Dore (white) a famous French grape grown a lot in Alsace; and Pinot Noir, a black grape which does need some shelter.

MAY

FLOWERS AND SHRUBS

Plant out annuals started under glass. Thin out annuals sown direct. Buy bedding plants towards the end of the month. Clear beds of spring bedding. Tie back daffodils or lift them and heel in a spare patch of ground to die back. Apply fertilizer, to prepare for bedding plants. Sow biennials like wallflowers and forget-me-nots for next year. Towards the end of the month plant up tubs, hanging baskets and window boxes. Spray roses against aphids and black spot. Plant chrysanthemums from the greenhouse, stopping the tips. Plant out dahlia tubers. Stake tall plants like delphiniums. Mulch established shallow-rooting shrubs like camellias and azaleas.

VEGETABLES, FRUIT AND HERBS

Plant outdoor tomato plants at the end of the month. Continue successive sowings of lettuce, carrots, spinach, beetroot, radishes and peas. Earth up early potatoes. Remove blossoms from strawberry runners in their first year. Sow French and runner beans in a prepared bed. Also sow kale and cabbage. Spray broad beans against blackfly. Spray cane fruits before they flower to prevent cane spot, and spray gooseberries against mildew. Spray apples and pears against scab. Plant out Brussels sprouts. Keep sowing parsley. Take cuttings of rosemary, sage and thyme. Plant out new herb garden. Put out slug pellets.

PLANTS UNDER PROTECTION

Begin to use shading and dampen the greenhouse when it gets hot. Ventilate in heat. Plant out half hardy annuals in boxes to plant outdoors in late May or early June. Plant cucumbers and greenhouse tomatoes in beds or gro-bags. Sow cinerarias to flower next winter. Start giving liquid fertilizer to greenhouse plants.

BEWARE THE 'May Gap'. You do not have it? Then you are a wise and thoughtful gardener who has planned ahead or you are a lucky one who has inherited lilac trees, late flowering blossom, dazzling wisteria, drooping golden laburnum and above all rhododendrons and azaleas. The May Gap is that period between the spring bulbs – which have pretty much done their stuff by the end of April – and the summer flowering bedding plants, herbaceous plants and of course those standbys, the roses. Obvious gap fillers at this time, which you should remember to plant in the autumn, are wall-flowers and forget-me-nots.

Such is the desperation that the May Gap produces in some people that they pay out huge sums to get forced bedding plants so as to alleviate the overall green. The last hour of the Chelsea Flower Show, which is the horticultural highlight of this month, demonstrates this lack. When the bell goes, and many plants come up for sale, pande-monium breaks loose and respectable souls tear each other's hats off. For not only are some fine plants in the offing but back home the garden looks shamefully drear. I have tended to take my holiday after Chelsea in order to avoid that drab view.

Growing azaleas

Of course azaleas and rhododendrons are a wonderful answer to the 'Gap'. If you don't have the right kind of lime-free soil you can have a go by introducing other soil in tubs or in a specially dug area separated from the outside soil by polythene (see Camellias). Other-wise they are easy to grow, the evergreen varieties actually enjoying shade and the deciduous ones liking semi-sun or dappled shade. There is no need to prune them unless they get too large and it is best to do this after flowering.

They come in a thrilling variety of colours from the really rather garish reds and pinks to the immensely subtle soft pinks, apricots and salmons veering to white. One of the most breathtaking views at Sissinghurst Castle garden is the azalea walk. In a moment of brilliant inspiration, it was planted out with the soft apricot-coloured varieties and at their feet bloom thousands upon thousands of blue-bells, both coming out simultaneously as if on cue. In fact all azaleas are technically rhododendrons, although because the general public insists on dividing them, so does the nurseryman. Common rhododen-

[31]

drons are nearly all evergreen whereas most of the ones we know as azaleas are in fact deciduous. It is the deciduous varieties of exotic hybrid such as the pink *R. kaempferi* which produce some of the most brilliant flowers – in full bloom there are times when these can cover a shrub so thickly that you cannot make out any leaves.

As there are well over 2,000 varieties of rhododendron it is quite difficult to know where to begin. A good shrub catalogue (see Appendix VI) will help you a lot, for it is no good planning and then not being able to get what you want. Make sure you are getting varieties which will not grow into trees as they vary greatly in size from the small rockery varieties to the huge bushes more suited to a park than to your garden. A lovely early white one is Cunningham's White or perhaps you might like a version slightly blushed with primrose called Diane. Sappho has white flowers with a dark blotch. A pretty coral pink is Betty Wormald and a much softer pale pink is Gomer Waterer which has an interesting yellow inside. If you want a rich purple try Purple Splendour. I tend to go less for the glowing red shades, for unless they are very carefully planted the effect can be a bit too strong. But one brilliant carmine red is Madame de Bruin.

With azaleas you might try some of the Ghent hybrids which have fragrant long-tubed, honeysuckle-like flowers. Knaphill and Exbury hybrids have a heavenly range of colours and the Mollis azaleas bloom early this month before their leaves appear.

I love the soft rose-pink colours like Berryrose and the whites with just a touch of yellow such as Persil. But to make your final choice, either go garden visiting now – which is such a pleasure anyway – or take yourself off to the Chelsea Flower Show at the end of the month. There they are on display in an abundance and variety I could not begin to describe. What's more, it is there that the new varieties will be shown. And when it comes to new varieties rhododendron and azalea fanatics know no bounds. There is something obsessive about these plants. You either love them or you don't. And if you love them and have the right soil the scope is joyous.

Breaking in a greenhouse

There is a certain type of person known as the hi-fi bore. This breed, among which I number several of my friends, are at their happiest when holding forth – despite my glazed look – on the prowess of their stereo systems. When I recognized that same look in a friend's eyes one day, I realized that I had become a greenhouse bore. Just as the hi-fi freaks cannot fathom how you survive without quadra-phonic, so I cannot conceive of muddling through without my greenhouse.

If you have a little artificial heat in it you can start your seeds there from February. But if not you can at least start doing so a month ahead of those out of doors. Then, come May, you start planting the tomato plants, peppers and cucumbers which will feed you from July through until October if you get your timing right. It is also such a useful place to overwinter those tender plants which you might not be wise to risk outside. In a mild winter your geraniums might survive. But that is a risk you take. For in general to be totally safe you need a bit of heat.

Statistics show that over one and a half million households in the south of England now have greenhouses and the numbers are in-creasing every day. The industry is huge and every year new models appear in all imaginable shapes to suit your space and needs (beware of the delightful-looking hexagonal ones; there's precious little room to work inside).

Comparatively speaking they are very cheap. The advertisers will claim they save you pounds and that just by growing tomatoes, a greenhouse will pay for itself in two years. Certainly mine saves me pounds by protecting my geraniums in winter, my seedlings through the early spring and by giving me vegetables all summer. Of course they do take up space which might deter people with small gardens where space is at a premium. But surely the whole challenge of a small garden is to see how much variety you can get out of it at any par-ticular time. In achieving this goal the greenhouse is your great ally. Greenhouses are generally made of wood or aluminium and fall into four categories: the free-standing, oblong shapes most frequently seen, the lean-tos, the hexagonals which are becoming more popular and the solardomes. However elegant and fine their design, I have to admit that I have never found aluminium greenhouses visually appealing. While I accept that they are easier to maintain and let in more light than wooden ones, I think it's important that they should be at least partially screened from the house.

I vastly prefer the cedar-wood houses. They are more expensive and require maintenance, but to my mind this disadvantage is far outweighed by the fact that once the wood weathers a bit they will blend into your garden settings so much better than the aluminium ones. The wooden frame does, of course, cut down your light area and many people prefer their greenhouses to be glazed to the base.

By far the cheapest kind are the aluminium and polythene ones. I highly recommend these if you have a sheltered spot (the polythene tears in persistent high winds) and are prepared to change the polythene every two years or so. By and large, though, they are only useful for growing summer crops.

One thing you must be prepared for is the cleaning. Unless the greenhouse is kept free of disease it can become a breeding ground for pests and fungus. Every spring and autumn comes the dreadful day when, dressed as a sweep, you empty it out completely, wash everywhere with Jeyes fluid diluted with water and then systematically wash all your plant pots and utensils outside in the same solution. Stakes, too, are less likely to rot if washed like this.

If you have a small garden, erecting a greenhouse may mean losing half the vegetable patch. Or if you garden on a balcony you certainly have no space. However there is a wonderful solution in the new breed of houses which are more like 'greencupboards' and which many firms now produce. They tend to stand about six feet high, be about two feet six inches deep and about six feet wide. They have adjustable shelving so that on one side you can grow several lots of seeds and keep plants in pots while on the other you could have tall tomatoes in a gro-bag.

The advantage of these spacious glass cupboards is that with their aluminium sliding doors you never have to go inside. It does seem a waste that so much room in a greenhouse has to be left free for you to get in and work – or rather stew – there. The glass cupboard should be erected against a sunny wall. If this is a wall of your house, so much the better, for some of the heat from indoors will come through and it wouldn't be at all difficult to run some heating in from your domestic system.

Alternatively, you could erect a 'greencupboard' against one of your windows. Obviously, if you have a heavenly view this would be a waste and it would also cut out some light. On the other hand it could be wonderfully attractive, get a lot of heat from the house and act as a kind of double glazing to boot.

Bagged growing

Nowadays I cannot think how I managed before the gro-bag – that long polythene sack containing a rich peat-based compost which has become a regular feature of almost every greenhouse. Its great merit is its simplicity. You lay the bag on the ground in or out of the greenhouse and cut out a narrow oblong shape along the dotted lines shown. Then add two gallons of water and get planting. You then continue to water regularly, occasionally adding a drop of liquid fertilizer. In early May, in a cold greenhouse, I plant two bags with tomatoes – Pixie (a tough little bush) and Moneymaker, using four plants per bag. I later add Carter's Fruit and Marmande (Hurst's large continental variety).

For planting outdoors you should wait until after the last frosts – towards the end of May. This also applies to tender vegetables like cucumbers, aubergines, peppers, etc. (Some people grow saladings like lettuces and chives.) There are also smaller bags for kitchen window sills which are ideal for making little herb gardens. The advantages of gro-bags are clear. You need no special soil preparation, your plants are less prone to disease and they need less watering because the area of exposed peat is quite narrow. You won't get much of a crop if you use the same bag next year, but you can use the compost as a mulch.

Gro-bags have two snags, however. First, being shallow, it is difficult to stake plants. You can now buy a special free-standing stake called a gro-grid, but I preferred to use gro-bags against a wall solving the staking problem more cheaply with string. Secondly, once settled they are difficult to move without disturbing the plant's roots. So you cannot, as with tubs, start a plant under glass and then move it outdoors when the weather gets warmer or, as in my case, when the squash begins to take over the whole greenhouse.

The chemistry of gardening

Walking round one spring Horticultural Society Show I saw a nervous man buying a stephanotis from a busy nurserywoman. 'Do I feed it ?' he asked, staring in awe at the waxy, white buds and glossy leaves of this exotic house-plant. Indeed he must, she said. Emboldened, he suggested Baby Bio. 'Goodness,' she said, 'you'll need something with a higher potash content than that,' – and was on to her next customer.

She might as well have told him to feed it Horlicks. To put him out of his misery I explained that Baby Bio, being high on nitrogen, was first rate for foliage plants. But he could easily buy a special high-potash liquid feed to get the flowers blooming. Failing that, he might do as well using the liquid feed he put on his tomatoes which was bound to contain a lot. It is interesting that many people are very competent gardeners without having the foggiest idea of what really makes their plants tick.

The three most important chemicals your plants require in varying degrees are nitrogen, phosphorus and potash. Nitrogen gives growth in leaves and stems and is essential to all plants, especially leafy ones – from grass to cabbages. Peas and beans can pick some up from the air, but most plants get it through the roots. Dried blood is a good source. If your plants grow slowly and have pale, yellow leaves, the chances are they need more. It is easily leached from the soil by winter rain so it needs constant replenishment.

Phosphorus is essential for developing the root system, so crucial to plants, particularly to root crops like carrots and parsnips. It also helps to form good seeds and builds up resistance to disease. Bone-meal contains a high proportion and lasts a long time in the soil. Potash encourages the plant's cells and is particularly valuable for fruits and flowers and strengthens corms and tubers. It is vital for fruit crops, particularly tomatoes and soft fruit like strawberries and redcurrants, and rose fertilizers contain a lot. Wood ash is an obvious organic source and is a good fertilizer. Phostrogen also contains a high proportion.

You can now test your soil content. The easiest way is with those little soil test kits which, with their bottles and tubes, are fun for embryo chemists in the family. But for most of us a good balance is all we need. This comes organically in cow or horse manure which has nearly even amounts of all three elements and has the bonus of improving the soil consistency by adding humus. Inorganically, good old national Growmore – of war-time fame – is still one of the cheapest balanced fertilizers containing equal quantities of each. Put a handful round your shrubs and roses now.

The outdoor room

The view from my upper window across my neighbours' back gardens
is a varied and instructive sight. There are those who still regard this
valuable space as nothing more than a place to hang the washing and
exercise the cat, others whose sole interest is roses. The Greeks next
door grow exotic vegetables and giant dahlias, and I am invariably
trying to do ten things at once. The most successful space users are the
Greeks. They have erected a sturdy wooden pergola against the
kitchen wall leading some fifteen feet out, have grown sweet-smelling
white jasmine over it and have added some coloured lights for good
measure. Under the pergola are tables and chairs and numerous tubs
of vivid flowers. The rest of the garden becomes a small tomato
nursery when August arrives. On warm summer evenings Zorba
music wafts across the roof tops and you know the Greeks are yet
again having a party in the garden.

In mediterranean climes it is natural to use the garden as just
another room in your home. But even in colder climes we could use
it so much more than we do as a place to eat, drink, work or relax
and, of course, as a play area for children. This requires much
thought and some expense, though. The area must be well-lit and
yet private, beautiful yet functional.

If you plan to eat out a lot it's a sensible idea to have your eating
area near the kitchen. You will also want it secluded. So up goes some
fencing – either a good solid woven or weather-boarded wooden
fence or a rather less private wooden lattice fence up which climbing
plants can grow and through which the sun can filter.

You might also try partly covering the eating area with a pergola
on which you can grow rambling roses, honeysuckle and clematis.
But unless you are a real handyman you would need expert help.
The wooden posts must be anchored in firm concrete foundations
at least a foot deep and the wood must be regularly treated with
preservative. A good, wooden pergola can look wonderfully natural
once it has been up a year or two. On this attractive framework you
can also hang baskets containing trailing plants like geraniums and
convenient things like herbs.

It seems silly to have garden furniture that cannot live out all year,
so wood or painted ironwork seem the best solutions. In garden

centres I often get deeply depressed by miles of ugly plastic or painted metal furniture upholstered in garish colours guaranteed to clash with all natural vegetation – and at fancy prices, too. But you can find many ranges of good wooden furniture including a lot made from felled elm trees. These all need an annual treatment with Cuprinol or some other preservative like linseed oil.

In a town garden you may well want some more architectural decoration as well as flowers and shrubs. A statue or an attractive urn would provide an interesting focal point. You could, of course, feast your eyes on stone nymphs and shepherds, but only if your bank balance is much healthier than mine. Alternatively, tell your local junk or antique shop to keep a lookout for you. Many garden centres have a good range of Italian or Spanish terra cotta containers which would be a great addition to any garden.

Summer bedding

The last weekend in May marks the beginning of the big bed-out. Garden centres everywhere are packed with over-night plant fanciers paying through the nose for petunias and geraniums. But don't be put off by prices. There are cheaper plants to be had and if you are willing to wait a bit you can buy younger plants much cheaper. A little tray of six will have grown to a good size in a month or so.

Bedding plants are a marvellous source of instant colour and should, if well watered and regularly dead-headed, keep blooming through till September. Like many town people I use bedding plants entirely in containers – tubs, window boxes, hanging baskets, and so on. These are strategically placed so that they can be enjoyed from the house and can easily be watered every day in hot weather.

Window boxes

If you have only a window sill, window boxes will really cheer you from within and look welcoming from outside. There's quite a choice from the cheaper plastic ones which are light and perfectly pleasant to the ornate terra cotta type.

PLATE 1 SOME TOWN GARDENS.

PLATE 2 SPRING FAVOURITES.
From top left to right: *Tulipa tarda*; *Anemone blanda*; *Helleborus orientalis*; *Euphorbia epithymoides*; *Euphorbia characias*; *Iris stylosa*.

PLATE 3 SUMMER FAVOURITES.
From top left to right: Hemerocallis; Verbascum; *Hosta crispula*;
Alchemilla mollis; *Lilium auratum*; Agapanthus.

Remember – your big problem will always be moisture. No window box will get enough naturally in summer, so you must be prepared to water regularly, use a good moisture-holding compost and choose plants which don't mind dry conditions. Place drainage material (some pebbles or chips of pot) along the base of the box and then fill with compost. I use a mixture of Levingtons (which has a peaty texture) and John Innes No 2 with some bonemeal for long-term plant food mixed in. The compost must be renewed annually. For good results you will still have to use liquid plant food perhaps once a fortnight in high summer.

Now for the plants. It's plain to see that geraniums thrive in these cramped conditions. They hold water well and so won't wilt and die if neglected over the Bank Holiday. Similarly, silver-leafed plants all of which hail from lands with low rainfall will be happy. Try *Helichrysum petiolatum*, a trailing silver plant with delightful heart-shaped leaves, or *Senecio greyi* which forms quite a little bush but will eventually get too large and be transferred to a tub. The silver leaves set off the bright-coloured bedding plants beautifully.

I've always found antirrhinums (the short varieties) survive well, as do marigolds. I particularly like the little yellow French marigolds and one year planted their even smaller relatives *Tagetes signata pumila* which hang delightfully over the edges of the boxes.

Petunias do seem the ideal window box plant. Once they have got off to a good start they survive considerable neglect without giving up. I love the way their huge gentle-textured bell-like flowers flutter in the breeze and I love their amazing, generous colours. They form fine billowing shapes cascading here and there and softening the lines of any container. A good plant to grow with your petunias is cineraria. This is a delicate silver-leafed plant which if your garden is quite sheltered will probably last from year to year.

One bedding flower I am never without is the tobacco plant or nicotiana. These are wonderfully strong plants that grow to about two feet and smell magical. They will flower all summer until you have to steel yourself to pull them up in October to make way for spring bulbs. They look especially fine grouped in a herbaceous border, but I also find they do magnificently in tubs and during the drought soldiered on when many plants had fallen by the wayside. I grow the white variety from seed as they are difficult to come by. On the other hand most nurseries will sell you a box of mixed colours which range through soft pinks and mauves to deep purples and magenta. If you are lucky enough to find a nurseryman selling green ones, pounce while you can. These are a fascinating lime green, and a group of them will really stand out in a border.

Shady plants

Whatever the truth of the matter, I have always assumed that the English summers of Milton and Marvell were wonderfully hot affairs. Why else should shade have held such an allure? Marvell's idea of a garden as 'a green thought in a green shade' conjures up a deeply peaceful image.

Today, shade is less in fashion, sunny borders with gaily coloured flowers being more *de rigueur*. In fact a shady garden can be an infinitely beautiful and subtle thing with its powerful tones of green, yellow and white among which lie the occasional gentle pinks and blues. So, if your garden is largely in shade, don't be defeatist. There are hosts of plants which will relish that condition so long as you choose them correctly.

Very few town gardeners are without a shady patch: against the north wall, under a tree or because the sun is blocked by neighbouring buildings. There are differing types of shade: the permanent shade in dark corners which can be very dry or damp and mossy; the permanent shade which for most of us is the north border; and the shade under trees which can either be permanent (as under beech or sycamore) or dappled, under small-leaved trees like birch.

Either way, planting under trees is complicated by the competition between the tree roots and your plants for the same supply of food and water in the ground, so avoid putting large shrubs there. In all shady areas it is crucial to add humus to improve the soil.

Many shrubs thrive in the shade. One of my favourites is *Choisya ternata*, the glossy-leaved Mexican orange blossom which will put up with anything except extreme wind and exposure. Its white, sweet-smelling flowers come out in June and continue spasmodically through the summer. Another old friend is *Mahonia aquifolium*, an evergreen with glossy, holly-like leaves and long strands of yellow flowers; again, the smell is wonderful.

Camellias actually prefer morning shade (early sun can damage their flowers if frost is about) and the C. *japonica* and C. *williamsii* are recommended for shady borders. Again, the evergreen glossy leaves are a delight all year round. Other fine-leaved shrubs are *Skimmia japonica*, the viburnums – V. *davidii* and V. *tinus* – and *Prunus lauroceras*.

Roses, too, can be content in shade. Those recommended as particularly suitable by the Royal National Rose Society are Conrad Meyer, Danse du Feu, Gloire de Dijon, Hugh Dickson, Mme Alfred Carrière, Maigold and Paul's Lemon Pillar. Many of these, as climbers, will grow up a shady wall, as will the wonderful deep red Parkdirektor Riggers and Mme Grégoire Staechelin.

Other plants that like shade are the heavenly green alchemillas, the aconites, violas, irises and primulas, many hostas and weird green-flowered euphorbias which would make those south-facing gardeners envy us our shade. I have never really got 'into' hostas, but I gather that once you do, there is no end to it. They are those subtle green- or yellow-leaved plants which grow bushy and luxuriant: often beside streams but also in shady borders. As with most shady plants, the richer the soil, the better.

Hosta crispula has a large variegated leaf, the main part being vivid green with an edging of cream. *H. fortunei* Albopicta is the reverse – wonderful cream to yellow leaves outlined in green. *H. plantaginea* has lush, green leaves and, if you are lucky, produces beautifully scented white trumpet flowers in autumn. One of the boldest is *H. sieboldiana* which grows to two feet and has large, heavily-veined blue-grey leaves which, while magnificent in themselves, look even more startling when juxtaposed in a green flower arrangement.

A traditional shady number is *Polygonatum* (Solomon's Seal) with its tall arching branches of evenly placed leaves and little pendulous white flowers. The *falcatum* variety has red-tinted stems and a narrow white edge to its leaf.

A good climber for the north facing wall is *Hydrangea petiolaris*, which will achieve a considerable size and is extremely easy to grow from cuttings. Honeysuckle – or lonicera – will produce more flowers in a sunny spot, but most are quite happy on a north wall. Pyracantha is also ideal with its charming white flowers and vivid red berries. Hydrangeas themselves are happy in or out of shade as long as they get a good water supply. Another good bet is chaenomeles or flowering quince.

Herbaceous plants that prefer shade include that striking feathery tall flower, the astilbe, which grows in clumps of pinks and yellows and white. It can become quite tall and spectacular. Dot aquilegia or columbine on a north border and they will seed themselves as fast as the alchemilla. So will foxgloves which are a great boon in mid-summer. Later you will greatly appreciate the day lilies (hemero-callis) which are as happy in light shade as in sun and can come in very subtle yellows and pinks as well as the more common orange.

Other green favourites are hellebores. *Helleborus corsicus* has thrived on my north border. From January to June its apple-green clusters of flowers flourish, contrasting vividly with the glossy, dark green foliage. *H. niger* is, of course, the much-loved Christmas Rose. Its sister *H. orientalis* is the Lenten Rose which produces flowers in varying colours of white, green and purple.

Primulas are particularly special to me and if you have a shady spot that is also moist they will romp away. *Primula japonica*, with its pink, white or magneta flowers in candelabra formation on a long stem is a joy in spring. *P. florindae* looks like a huge cowslip while *P. bulleyana* has tall stems with many orange flowers. You can also grow *Lilium henryi*, *L. martagon*, tiger lilies and a good many more. Come evening, your shady nook will smell divine.

JUNE

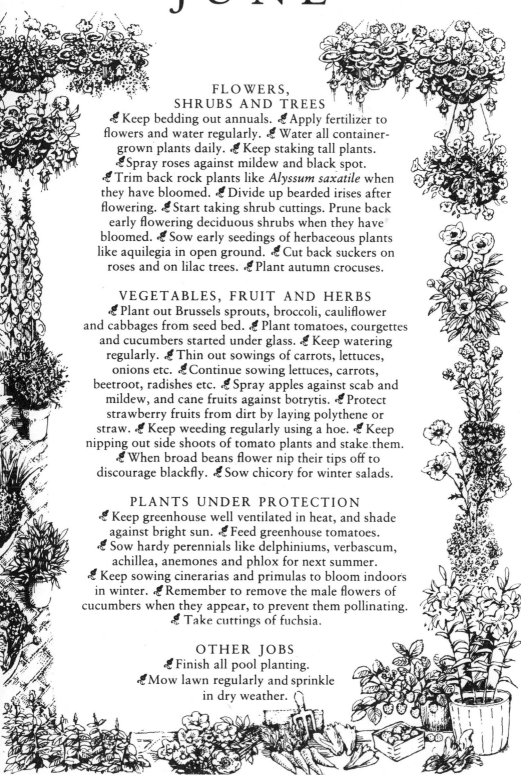

FLOWERS, SHRUBS AND TREES

Keep bedding out annuals. Apply fertilizer to flowers and water regularly. Water all container-grown plants daily. Keep staking tall plants. Spray roses against mildew and black spot. Trim back rock plants like *Alyssum saxatile* when they have bloomed. Divide up bearded irises after flowering. Start taking shrub cuttings. Prune back early flowering deciduous shrubs when they have bloomed. Sow early seedings of herbaceous plants like aquilegia in open ground. Cut back suckers on roses and on lilac trees. Plant autumn crocuses.

VEGETABLES, FRUIT AND HERBS

Plant out Brussels sprouts, broccoli, cauliflower and cabbages from seed bed. Plant tomatoes, courgettes and cucumbers started under glass. Keep watering regularly. Thin out sowings of carrots, lettuces, onions etc. Continue sowing lettuces, carrots, beetroot, radishes etc. Spray apples against scab and mildew, and cane fruits against botrytis. Protect strawberry fruits from dirt by laying polythene or straw. Keep weeding regularly using a hoe. Keep nipping out side shoots of tomato plants and stake them. When broad beans flower nip their tips off to discourage blackfly. Sow chicory for winter salads.

PLANTS UNDER PROTECTION

Keep greenhouse well ventilated in heat, and shade against bright sun. Feed greenhouse tomatoes. Sow hardy perennials like delphiniums, verbascum, achillea, anemones and phlox for next summer. Keep sowing cinerarias and primulas to bloom indoors in winter. Remember to remove the male flowers of cucumbers when they appear, to prevent them pollinating. Take cuttings of fuchsia.

OTHER JOBS

Finish all pool planting. Mow lawn regularly and sprinkle in dry weather.

THIS MUST BE the most rewarding month in a gardener's year. It must also, I think as I garden until darkness sends me indoors around ten o'clock, be the most pleasurable. Those long June evenings which you can spend either sitting with friends in the garden admiring the fruits of your labours with all senses alive – that smell of Albertine rose mingling with the opening philadelphus is too good to be true – or weeding and bedding out, are guaranteed to bring a calm and tranquillity to your life. Little seems *that* important – the office rows, the things you have left undone – as nature's rhythm takes over.

Those long gardening evenings are a particularly British thing. The most tight-lipped of neighbours start talking over the garden fence, admiring that peony which for years has sulked but has suddenly stunned the street with its exotic white blooms, or exchanging tips or cuttings.

Peonies

It is the peonies which always succeed in bowling me over in June. If you have none you should really make a space for them because even their quite short life is to me worth any rose which blooms all summer. They hail variously from China, Tibet and parts of Europe, and over the years have so intoxicated us that many hundreds of hybrids have been created, varying from the single-petalled varieties like Bowl of Beauty with their generous, tufty yellow centres, to the great round heads made up of more petals than you could count. They range in colour from brilliant white through soft pinks, creams and yellows to vivid crimson and deep, deep velvety wine colours.

Just in case you have not got the message: they take my breath away. I can never believe they are quite true. Notcutts' catalogue compiler – on whom they clearly have the same effect – describes them as 'a class by themselves'. They are 'a vice-less family – no staking, no periodic lifting, good foliage, particularly in spring and autumn; weed-suppressing', to which list I might add they don't mind blooming in dappled (though not deep) shade, which is always a plus in a town garden.

You should also remember that they do not like to be moved about so when you plant them you should prepare the soil with lots of compost and fertilizer. Then every year when the leaves die down give them a good covering of manure to feed next year's growth. Of course in the winter your peony bed will be drab, but come spring the distinctive deep pink spikes will begin to appear. A friend of mine had the brilliant idea of planting his peony bed for spring. In March the bed is a vivid blue as the hundred or so scilla bulbs which he planted along with the peonies burst into flower, and when they die back the peonies are on the way.

There are varieties that bloom as early as May so you may wish to spread your season over three months. My favourite May bloomer is the unusual *P. mlokosewitschii*. This is a beautiful species from the Caucasus which bears large cup-shaped flowers with lemon-yellow, open petals and deep, deep golden stamens. The flowers do not last for long, but there are many of them and they will thrill you during their short life.

To choose your June and July flowering varieties get hold of a specialist catalogue such as Kelways' which gives helpful illustrations. Bowl of Beauty is always easy to find. It has the exotic mix of sugar-pink petals and soft yellow stamens. Of the double varieties Claire Dubois is the silvery shell pink you associate with the rose New Dawn. Albert Crousse is a mite deeper but still touchingly soft. Mme Emilie Lemoine is a sharp ivory white which will gleam out on a dreary day whereas Duchesse de Nemours has just a hint of cream. Sarah Bernhardt is the pink of apple blossom. Then you get to the almost vulgar rich pinks of Magic Orb and President Poincare and to the deep red shades such as King Arthur and King of England; these last two are what is known as Imperial peonies in which the stamens have been so developed that a single peony appears almost double.

As if this is not enough you could, if space is available, grow a tree peony. These are not often grown and I can't think why for they are extremely hardy and unfussy about soil, and will grow well over five feet with excellent foliage if left to themselves. Some come smaller and you could choose one of these if you lack space. *P. suffruticosa* is the best garden variety. Their names are suitably aristocratic: Duchess of Marlborough is a deep rose pink, Countess of Crewe is paler and Lord Shelbourne is a lovely pale salmon pink. A rather odd and exciting one is Souvenir du Maxime Cornu which is a golden yellow with the feathery petals just edged with carmine – to my mind the loveliest of all.

Urban farming

As a quick zip around your local garden centre or a trip to the corner shop will prove, it is now high time to plant out the less hardy vegetables like tomatoes, cucumbers and peppers which have been forced under glass. The shops are full of them. They seem ludicrously dear when for a tenth of the price you could have grown them from seed. But this is no time for regrets. A tub or gro-bag placed on a pocket-handkerchief-sized balcony or window sill, or indeed in a sunny space indoors, could bring in a small harvest.

Sages who tell you that by growing home vegetables in tubs you will be able to combat food prices are talking hokum, and also missing the point. By the time you have paid for the gro-bag, the plant and the fertilizer, not to mention your time, it is scarcely a bargain. What is more, just when your tomatoes ripen those in the shops will probably be cheap. However, there is no shadow of doubt that yours, fresh from the pot, will taste infinitely more delicious. As for the satisfaction you will get, there is no way to quantify it.

For some delicious salads in August I suggest you plant tomatoes, peppers, cucumbers and perhaps lettuces, all of which will look attractive and thrive in tubs ten inches across filled with a good potting compost. And of course you should never be without herbs which grow well in window boxes. Chives are easy to grow and will spread fast, dying down in winter but returning more vigorously next year. Basil can be touchy even in summer, needing a really warm window sill, and will die, come the cold. However, it is one of the most pleasant and aromatic additions to any tomato salad.

I grow sorrel in a plastic tub on the balcony. It flourishes from year to year. One leaf chopped up thinly can transform a dull salad and it is a marvellous soup ingredient. You can never have enough parsley – and new potatoes without mint (which should be grown in a pot on its own) are hardly worth eating. Nor should you be without tarragon, sage, thyme and rosemary which will stick by you from year to year.

Most vegetables have some snags. With peppers you should nip out the growing tip once some flowers have formed or the fruit will be meagre. With cucumbers the problem is their sex life. Unlike courgettes, where you frantically attempt to get the male and female flowers to pollinate (female flowers are identified by the little bulge behind the flower), with cucumbers this should not be permitted or they will turn bitter.

The snag with tomatoes is that most varieties must be constantly pruned by nipping out their side shoots which somehow steal a march on you. However this problem does not occur with bush varieties, so out of sheer laziness I recommend growing bush tomatoes. They hardly need staking since they spill over the edge of the tub or bag, and really add to their surroundings.

You ought now to be thinking of planting vegetables to eat in autumn and winter – among them, carrots, beetroot, spinach, endive and chicory. You should also be transplanting your broccoli and Brussels sprouts plants from the seed bed. Be wary of buying plants from garden centres because you could import club root – a vile disease, carried in the soil, which attacks brassicas (broccoli, Brussels sprouts, cabbage, cauliflower and kale) and is the devil to get rid of.

By now the snails should be out in force. So beware. They are particularly happy in the wettest summer weather and that is when you can catch them making short work of your courgette plants. Slug pellets are the answer, or – if you feel like a nocturnal onslaught – go out with your torch and salt cellar before turning in and catch them red-handed. Salt kills fast. You may also have trouble with cabbage root fly which again goes for all brassicas. However, you can combat this by using a soil pesticide like Bromophos when you plant.

Its important to keep feeding your crops. They need all the help they can get, particularly if you are on poor soil and don't have manure readily available. I spread Growmore and rake it into the soil. But the experts tend to suggest weekly liquid feeds with chemicals like Phostrogen. I use this in my flower tubs and the difference it makes is terrific.

Office vegetables

For a last thought about vegetables, have you ever thought of growing them in the office? If your sandwiches are getting boring and that daily yoghurt is beginning to pall, why not liven up your lunch hour with a touch of home-grown – or office-grown – food? The chances are you have a very small amount of space and light. But there's bound to be enough for a pot of chives (to give that yoghurt a lift) or some other tasty herb like summer savory or marjoram to cheer up your sandwich.

Growing food in the office is easy, but it can be unpopular. Before you begin, make sure you have enough trays or saucers on which to stand your containers. That way there is no chance of soil getting on the typewriter or dirty water running through to your neighbour's files. A particularly good container, if you have the full run of a window sill, is one of those elegant-looking plastic window boxes for which you can buy a specially made tray. But first, what to grow? As a child you no doubt grew mustard and cress on blotting paper and it's still as easy to do now. Sprinkle the seeds on damp blotting paper or a thick absorbent cloth in a shallow tray. An ideal container is the sort of tray you get in garden centres which does not have holes in the bottom (it is meant to hold little pots). For this you can get a propagator lid, which means there is less chance of your cress drying up over the weekend, if it is kept out of the sun.

Sprouting beans in jars is also easy and clean and will add greatly to your sandwiches. You can buy them in health food shops or garden centres. The can be grown in a jam jar with muslin over the top. You might start them off at home as they must be washed out once a day.

Of the herbs, you can easily buy chives in a garden centre or grow them from seed. They last very happily in pots and add to any salad or sandwich. Mint grows well anywhere, and will flourish in pots. Anyone who likes Greek food knows that mint goes wonderfully with plain yoghurt. Just take a root from your garden or from a friend.

Another very tasty herb which needs a sunny spot is sweet basil. You can grow it from seed in the warm, or buy plants. It chops up beautifully with tomatoes and has the added attraction of smelling exotic. Marjoram and sweet savory are interesting new tastes, and sorrel – which needs regular watering – is strong and very tasty.

When it comes to larger plants the two obvious ones are tomatoes and peppers. Both can look very attractive on a window ledge in a large pot – particularly peppers. Tomatoes can get out of hand, especially if they do not have much light, so choose the small fruiting bush varieties which keep to a sensible shape and do not need the side shoots nipped out. Peppers are more manageable and when the fruits turn red they can look as pretty as any pot plant.

Hang up your plants

By now you will have got your window boxes all bedded out on the window sill or patio (see May) but something is still lacking. Everything is blooming at foot or waist level, and a hanging basket can change that perspective. I am something of a hanging basket freak. It can become a trial since they need so much watering, but nothing could look more charming than the ones that hang from my apple tree trailing rather out-of-control petunias, or those which hang from the pergola framing the view and trailing silver *Helichrysum petiolatum* in a distinctly romantic way.

There are various sorts of hanging basket. The cheapest and most common are the wire ones, now often covered in plastic, which you line with moss, then line with polythene on the bottom to stop all the water running out or evaporating. You plant them just like a tub or window box, but with emphasis, of course, on things that trail down. The best plants of all for this are the ivy-leafed hanging geraniums which have the added advantage of putting up with a lot of drought. You can also punch little holes in your polythene and plant your trailing alyssum and lobelia in those so that plants grow from all parts of the basket.

I find the wire baskets very difficult to keep moist and they are often not terribly attractive. So instead I get handsome plastic pots of a shallow kind, perhaps with a little round tray to catch some of the water that flows out. Your plants will, in my experience, grow so fast in these that you will soon not see the plastic basket. You can buy them ready set up as hanging baskets or make up your own. In America I discovered a gadget which they call a 'hang-up' which is simply four lengths of strong nylon thread joined with a ring at one end and a two-inch square perspex base at the other. You place your basket or bowl on the base, hang it up and it appears to float unaided. An alternative are the nylon string plant-hangers which are available in many shops.

When it comes to the plants remember that those little tagetes combined with a good mix of petunias, trailing lobelias, alyssum and pelargoniums or perhaps some dwarf antirrhinums combined with some silver plants like *Helichrysum petiolatum* or *Senecio cineraria* (Silver Dust), will look a joy. But unless they are watered every evening in hot weather, and quite regularly come hail or shine, most plants will die away, leaving just the pelargoniums to muddle through.

In high summer it would pay off to add some liquid feed to your water about once a fortnight. Within a day or two you can see the difference. I use Phostrogen as a good standby, but there are many other chemicals and liquid manures to choose from.

New York interlude

'Ever wondered what the hell to do with all your used tennis balls?' said a New York motor millionaire as he showed me his penthouse roof garden overlooking Park Avenue. No, I said, too bashful to admit that a glut of tennis balls had never been my problem. He went on to tell me that they were ideal for putting in the bottom of tubs, under the soil. They provided good drainage and, being full of air, made the tub lighter – so important on a roof. Now word is out I've no doubt the market price of old tennis balls will soar as New Yorkers grasp the latest gardening fad. Roof-top gardening is serious stuff for them – and their experience offers some useful lessons for us.

Take the elevator to the top floor of any high-rise block and all round you you'll see a patchwork of tiny, bushy gardens wherever there is a spare foot. From the street below they look like bizarre hairy growths on the otherwise totally smooth body of a skyscraper. Though there have always been rich people with penthouses and balconies full of flowers the craze for gardens in the sky is comparatively new. In 1977 New York Magazine referred to 'the city's great untapped resource: 20,000 acres of roof-tops – enough usable space to hold Central Park twenty-three times over'.

As with any city roof there are minor hitches like planning regulations – not a problem if everything is mobile – and weight. It is important to stand tubs at the side of a roof to avoid stress. New York also has a much greater heat problem than London, so elaborate watering systems are installed which allow you to go away for a day or two in July without the whole thing drying up. Wood chips are much used as a mulch to retain water.

Roof protection can be a major snag and New Yorkers often lay down attractive wooden decking which protects the surface and distributes some of the stress caused by the tubs. Another favourite cover is Astroturf (plastic grass) which both protects the roof and gives it a grassy look. I was surprised how nice it could look as a background. A more permanent favourite is terra cotta tiles which look warm and do not weigh much. It is never a good scheme to put earth directly onto the roof; it harms the asphalt and if the roof springs a leak the whole bed must be dug up. So plastic sheeting merchants are doing a brisk business.

Evergreen shrubs and trees are naturally popular, looking reasonable all year round. In summer out come the annuals, and roof gardeners compete for the most colourful mix of pansies, petunias, busy lizzie, lobelia and begonias (this is known as The English Garden Look).

My friend of tennis ball fame was more original. His stock was entirely grown from seed under artificial lighting in the large but cluttered penthouse, and most of it was edible. As we walked round I nibbled all sorts of herbs and an interesting mix of leafy lettuces (from wine red to lime yellow) and saw marrow, tomatoes and sweet corn (all sun lovers) coming on well. The runner beans had made a good start up the fruit trees. From a special hydroponic unit Chinese cabbage sprouted, unusual and tasty. The seeds for the cabbage, the interesting mustard greens and the water spinach all came from Hong Kong. This huge array of tubs was raised on breeze blocks to make picking easier and the effect prettier. I remarked to my friend that in his busy life this must take up a lot of time, and he conceded that his several gardeners *were* a boon . . . .

Miniature roses

Gardeners with tiny patches who want to make the most of them could do a lot worse than think of planting miniature roses. To my mind they look rather silly as edging plants in large beds, but given a proper place to themselves, as they are in the sunken garden at the Royal National Rose Society's St Albans grounds, they can look very special. I first visited the sunken garden late one June. The experience, after being surrounded by good-sized roses, is really magical. Suddenly – Gulliver-like – you are among the little people.

The sunken garden is entirely given over to miniature roses arranged on three levels, along with some interesting ground cover foliage plants which always add variety of texture in a rose garden. Few of the roses can be more than twelve inches tall and their tiny flowers vary from deep red and pink, through the mixed yellow-pink of Masquerade to the softer shades and the glorious little whites. In and amongst them are standard miniature roses rising to all of two feet.

Having never given much time to miniature roses, this was an eye-opener. It also made me think that many town gardeners, with their limited space, could get immense pleasure from growing miniatures which – given the right conditions – can grow to little bushes up to sixteen inches tall and give several crops of flowers a year.

My enthusiasm is in no way original. Interest in miniature roses is fast increasing and most rose catalogues, such as Cant's and Mattock's, have a good selection. The biggest supplier of miniatures is Gregory's Roses who have produced Green Diamond, the first-ever green miniature, whose tiny double lime flowers must be a godsend to flower arrangers. They have also introduced Dresden Doll, the first miniature moss rose, in a soft salmony pink.

You can grow miniatures in various ways: as a complete miniature rose garden, or part of a mixed miniature garden, in window boxes and tubs, or simply as edging plants on a mixed border where they will provide colour as long as any plant. They can also appear in rockeries, but, being true roses, they need a good, cool, moist root-run and will not relish being brought indoors for long.

Some specially pretty varieties are Cinderella, with a charming white flower; Pixie, which is soft pink; Stacey Sue, with its sugar pink blooms; Pour Toi, a cream-coloured, bushy rose; Eleanor, a glowing apricot pink; Rosina, bright, creamy yellow; and Rosmarin, a more vivid pink. A bed of miniatures will not be cheap and you will need about four to fill the space taken by an average rose.

There are many small roses which, while not technically miniatures, should suit you if you are short on space. For example, Harkness list many floribundas (Tip Top, Marlena, Kim, Stargazer etc.) which only reach eighteen inches on average and look fine in a low border. Then there are the slightly taller, small-flowered shrubs which I grow and love, such as Little White Pet, which will produce a profusion of double white flowers for months.

The final revelation of the sunken garden was the Nozomi Rose. This Japanese introduction is ideal for ground cover or for cascading over a wall or over the sides of an urn. Its prostrate branches grow several feet forming a mat of thousands of the most enchanting little single pink flowers which last a good eight weeks through the summer.

The friendly weed

From my childhood I remember our front lawn not just as a source of endless daisy chains but also as the home of hosts of intoxicating tiny flowers. Tormentil, bird's foot trefoil, milkwort, speedwell, tiny clovers and yellow and scarlet pimpernel could all be found. This would, of course, be anathema to the seed and fertilizer merchants whose advertisements for particular brands of lawn seed and fertilizer show a flat green lawn quite uninfected by 'weeds'. All so unlike our own dear family lawn.

As one who still delights in daisies and is pleased to greet a speedwell flowering in the border (for, after all, what is a weed but a wild flower in the wrong spot?) I was thrilled to meet a gentleman who was bold enough to actually exhibit weeds at the Chelsea Flower Show. He was from the Soil Association and some joker had placed his stand, for the third year running, opposite the Weed Research Organisation which is dedicated to the control of weeds. Not that the Soil Association promotes the uncontrolled use of weeds. But its booklet *The Value of Weeds* outlines their uses as indicators of the state of your soil, as soil conditioners and, most important, as valuable providers of nutrients to your plants both via the compost heap (the Association also produces an excellent booklet on compost making) and through liquid fertilizers.

Did you know, for example, that the stinging nettle can be a blessing? It contains much nitrogen and can thus stimulate growth in other plants – particularly soft fruit – if allowed to flourish nearby. It breaks down into excellent humus, instantly raising the temperature of your compost heap. Nettles also make a good mulch between vegetable rows. If you soak a bunch of fresh nettles in rainwater for two to three weeks you will have a smelly but efficient liquid fertilizer particularly suited to tomatoes. An infusion made from a handful of fresh nettles boiled in a pint of water and left to cool can be mixed with four parts water and used as a spray against mildew, blackfly, aphids and plant lice – in addition to its value as a foliar feed.

You can make a good natural liquid manure by steeping mixed weeds in a bucket of rainwater for a couple of weeks. This returns all the excellent nutrients to your plants. Another useful ploy is to allow weeds to develop in your onion bed when the onions are getting to a good size. By thus depriving them of nitrogen you increase their ability to keep. When you have harvested the onions dig the weeds back into the soil. Weeds also provide some cover in the winter, protecting the soil from weathering. To the Soil Association the greatest sacrilege is to burn or kill your weeds. So if you see your neighbour innocently spraying venomous chemicals on his nettlebed you could give him the *good* news about weeds!

Pests

Some people have nightmares about finding cockroaches in their shoes. I am equally illogical about greenfly. The very thought of inadvertently touching a bloom and getting covered with thousands of squashed greenflies makes me turn as green as the pests themselves. We rightly associate aphids or greenfly (there are 500 recorded species and they also come in pink or black) with roses. But they can cluster on other plants – they especially love tulips – and are particularly unpleasant to discover if you've brought flowers into the house. Whiteflies breed daily on your tomatoes and are also insidious. They don't kill outright, but will weaken the plant and deplete your stock.

Of course, with many of the numerous garden pests and diseases, prevention is the best cure. If you empty your greenhouse and fumigate it in spring and autumn, washing the glass with Jeyes fluid and warm water, you are less likely to fall prey to the pests and mould which might otherwise settle in.

Insecticides control pests in two ways: killing them outright by leaving a deposit which the insects eat, or being absorbed into the plant so that plant-sucking pests – notably aphids – die when sucking the sap. Names of insecticides can be confusing, each firm giving a more deadly name to the same chemical. But remember, insecticides are only a help if you follow the instructions carefully. An overdose can kill the plant itself, as could a mixture of two sprays.

Plants for dry weather

Any devotee of the Chelsea Flower Show cannot have failed to notice Beth Chatto, that small, merry lady who every year brings van loads of unusual plants up from Essex to form a mini-Eden somewhere in the big tent. We all crowd around wishing we could produce such subtle and brilliant effects back home. One year I remember she devoted one section to the wet garden – back home she has a stream area where marshy plants can flourish – and another to the dry garden, which is so appropriate to East Anglia. She has even written a book on dry gardens.

'I really don't hold with watering,' she writes, which seems odd for a start. But after reading her book I did realize that if I followed her regime both by nurturing my soil in the first place and constantly replenishing it, and by selecting just the right plants, I might also be in a position to make such airy remarks.

Beth Chatto lives and has a thriving nursery at Elmstead Market near Colchester – an area whose rainfall must be among the lowest in the country. Her soil sounds nothing to write home about, yet she has managed to create one of the most interesting gardens you can visit.

I was particularly drawn to her book because if something can survive in a dry garden either in sun or shade, it stands to reason that – size permitting – it would probably flourish in tubs. I am a relentless waterer of over 40 tubs and nearly went bananas in the 1976 drought, so any tip I can glean is a boon. I'm sure that many of you are in the same position and would do a lot to avoid witnessing those tragic deaths which invariably take place when you gaily disappear for the summer holidays.

Getting your soil right is, of course, half the battle. The more humus and fibrous material it contains, the better it will retain water. So a successful compost heap is crucial to Beth Chatto's recipe – failing that, rotted manure or peat. This should be dug in during the autumn over the whole soil area and is particularly important when you are creating a new flower bed.

Ground cover is the next ingredient. There are many enchanting low-lying plants like stachys, small hebes, lamiums, helianthemums and bergenias which will round out into a lovely clumpy ground cover at quite a rate. But whenever there is no natural cover a good mulch of straw, peat, lawn mowings or the wood chippings that Beth uses will really help. Remember, it is important not to mulch until the ground is heavily saturated.

When it comes to drought-resistant flora, many of Beth Chatto's favourites are my own. She loves silver-leaved plants, like the artemisias which range from low growing varieties to the large feathery-leaved *A. arborescens*, and swears by senecio, sedums, rue and santolinas. These she contrasts with darker leaves like those of the cistus or rock rose which, coming from southern Europe, are used to low rainfall.

Other favourites are those positively primeval-looking green flowers – the euphorbias. These come in many shapes and sizes with flowers ranging from dark green with black markings through lime to yellow, and are thus a flower arranger's dream. The largest, *E. characias wulfenii*, can grow up to six feet high and would be the star of any herbaceous border, while *E. polychroma* forms a wonderful dome about twelve inches high covered with golden yellow heads for several months in spring.

Beth Chatto believes that garden plans should be made from shapes and sizes rather than colours. She includes some intriguing schemes from her own garden where soft rounded shapes are juxtaposed with exotic verticals like *Iris foetidissima* or the huge yucca with its cactus-like rosette of leaves and immense flower spikes reaching to eight feet, or the *Acanthus mollis latifolius* which grows widely-cut spreading leaves and five-foot spikes. I mention these last, for to use them you must first find yourself a large herbaceous border.

JULY

FLOWERS AND SHRUBS

Water flowers in tubs every day. Take cuttings of hardy shrubs like hebe, *Senecio greyi* and lavender. Regularly deadhead annuals like petunias to encourage flowers. Deadhead and feed roses. Collect seeds of plants you wish to propagate. When delphiniums fade cut them to ground level. Mulch around shrubs and roses. Sow seeds of perennials like lupins and delphiniums. Plant out wallflower and forget-me-not seedlings. Be sure chrysanthemums and dahlias are well staked. Keep cutting sweet peas to encourage more flowers. Prune rambler roses, weigela and philadelphus after flowering. Dry flowers for winter decorations.

VEGETABLES, FRUIT AND HERBS

Keep watering and feeding vegetables regularly. Tomatoes need a weekly feed. Sow winter lettuce, spinach, cabbage and winter radishes. Plant out your leeks and earth up those planted last month. Sow French beans. Continue planting out broccoli, Brussels sprouts and cabbage from the seed bed. Spray against woolly aphids on fruit trees. Remove unwanted runners in your strawberry bed and layer runners you wish to retain. Throw out plants that have cropped 3 summers. Cut herbs for drying or freezing. Sow more parsley.

PLANTS UNDER PROTECTION

Take cuttings of hardy shrubs like camellias and elaeagnus. Take cuttings of clematis and geraniums using sandy compost. Spray house-plants with water, also feed them. Feed tomatoes, cucumbers and peppers regularly. Remove male flowers of cucumbers and side shoots of tomatoes. Spray regularly against whitefly and red spider mite.

OTHER JOBS

Mow the lawn regularly and sprinkle in peat. Use selective weedkillers. Make sure the water level remains constant in your pool. Do construction jobs while the weather holds.

EVERY WEEKEND in high summer when I go out into the country I make a point of visiting some garden that is open to the public. If I stay in town to weed my own I still take some time off to go looking. For only that way can you really learn what no book can teach: the art of using your imagination with plants. Before I gardened I used to paint a lot. Now I no longer feel the urge, for what little creativity I have can go into the flowerbeds. Our island is full of garden artists, as country villages in July testify. But there are some real greats who make the rest of us look mere Sunday painters. Gardens like Hidcote, planned and planted by Lawrence Johnson, and Sissinghurst, created by Vita Sackville-West are the work of true artists. So in this day is Barnsley House, Rosemary Verey's magical garden near Cirencester, or Nymans in Sussex.

A good gardener is always looking for ways to perfect his garden. So however busy you are in your own, do go looking. Keep those guidebooks in the car along with the yellow book issued by the National Gardens Scheme (see Appendix VII) which comes out annually to tell you which private gardens are opening in aid of charity on a Sunday afternoon, so that wherever you find yourself there is always somewhere you can drop in for an hour on the way home. Usually the owner or gardener is around to answer your questions about unusual plants. Often there are rare plants to buy so that your own garden will become a mass of souvenirs from happy weekends.

Yellow gardens

It was at Barnsley that I learned to love verbascums – those amazing tall spikey plants with furry stems and leaves. They produce along their spikes hundreds of flowers, but with never more than a handful fully open at once so that as the petals fall more flowers open and the bloom lasts from June until August. The primrose yellow V. Gainsborough is my favourite for I adore that colour, but there are white and soft pink varieties too. I become so accustomed to their loveliness this month that I feel I shall weep when they finally die back.

Barnsley's verbascums are huge and are an essential part of the scheme of blues, yellows and whites which in July is the garden's main feature, with its mass of frothing alchemilla, lovely clumps of yellow fererfew, delphiniums and – a touch of brilliance – a deep blue *Clematis alpina* growing in a yellow privet bush. Barnsley's laburnum walk in spring – now famed as the cover of *The English-woman's Garden* – is a classic example of the marvellous mixture of blues and mauves with yellow.

Another wonderful yellow and blue garden is at Hidcote. Much of Hidcote consists of small gardens surrounded by high hedges and linked in such a way that one is continually surprised. Mrs Winthrop's Garden is a tiny square sloping garden surrounded by beech, horn-beam and lime hedges. All the plants (with the exception of the copper-coloured cordylines which stand in tubs making a striking architectural contrast) are in shades of blue and yellow.

Round the path edges froths yellow-green *Alchemilla mollis*, cheek by jowl with the blue and yellow flowers of rue. Creeping yellow ground cover is provided by yellow-leafed origano, and little blue violas and campanulas grow in and amongst it.

The shrubs nearly all have yellow variegated leaves and include brilliant *Elaeagnus pungens* Maculata, *Diervilla florida variegata*, a honeysuckle called Baggesen's Gold, *Euonymus fortunei* and variegated holly. *Yucca gloriosa variegata* with their striped spiky forms break up the softer lines. There are also yellow lilies, yellow-leafed hostas and hops, yellow-leafed sage and tall blue delphiniums and campanulas. In early summer there are yellow peonies.

Another shrub for which Hidcote is famous is the Hidcote hyperi-cum. I generally find hypericum a little too vividly yellow, but blend-ing with softer shades it looks wonderful and makes a welcome splash of colour in August. It also appears to manage well in shade.

Of course, there is great advantage in a garden which depends a lot for its character on the colour of its foliage, for long after the flowers have gone it will flourish and look lovely in the winter.

Roses old and new

Whatever else I see, the things that I think of most in July are roses. For it is now that they all flower with a burst – the old-fashioned ones which will only come out once and so must be treasured so much the more, and the faithful modern ones; the hybrid teas and floribundas which have a place in everyone's garden (see August). Although I never believe in growing roses on their own in a rose garden as it looks like death in winter and, besides, they mix so well with other things, I do love visiting special rose gardens in July. The Royal National Rose Society's gardens near St Albans are a good example for there you can see over 1,000 roses. (For climbers see February.)

Reading the Rose Society list of varieties is like studying a race card: Chinatown, bred by Poulsen out of Columbine and Clare Grammerstorf; Galway Bay, bred by McGrady out of Heidelberg and Queen Elizabeth. What comes as a surprise is that these two roses – regular features of rose catalogues and particular favourites of mine – were only bred in 1963 and 1966 respectively.

Although roses decorate the borders of Renaissance paintings and feature widely in literature, these are not the roses of our suburban gardens. With one exception (my namesake, the little white rambler Félicité et Perpetué which dates from 1827) the roses in my garden were bred within the last hundred years, and most much more recently.

When Reynolds Hole and Honeywood D'Ombrain, two Victorian parsons, founded the National Rose Society in 1876, the rose world was in ferment. The hybrid tea, that standard feature of all modern gardens, had just been invented. The first was La France in 1867 and it emerged from the breeding of a hybrid perpetual with a rose imported from China. The Victorian hybrid perpetuals were developed from the Bourbon rose which itself was the result of cross-breeding in 1817 between other Chinese imports and Damask roses.

Ever since then rose breeders like Meilland in France, Tantau and Kordes in Germany, Dickson in Northern Ireland and Harkness in England have continued in their experiments in search of an ever more perfect rose. When I once asked Jack Harkness why he had not named a rose after his wife he replied that he would need to breed a perfect rose; and the perfect rose is always to come next year. So every year new creations appear from the breeders who are showing their wares at Chelsea; some garish and not to my taste but no doubt ideally long-flowering, others thrilling and timeless.

There is a kind of person called the rose snob who will only wish to plant the more subtle old-fashioned roses. But to do this you must have lots of space – for old shrub roses can grow so tall and wide – and also be able to turn your back on them for the many months that they do not flower. So in a small garden the trick is to grow a mix of the old and the new so that you are never without roses.

Some of the oldest roses are the albas such as Felicité Parmentier which make fine shrubs with handsome leaves, but which only flower in summer. Then there are the centifolias or cabbage roses which include among them one of my very favourites, Fantin-Latour, which has deep pink buds and opens to a perfect blush-pink flower with its many petals crushed together like a cabbage; it seems to come straight out of a painting. Like the albas they will also make good hedges.

The ideal hedging roses are the rugosas. This breed of loosely formed, open flowers on marvellously leafy bushes are justly loved. They include in their number some of the most popular and romantic of roses like Roseraie de l'Hay which has a vivid purple flower with a magnificent scent, lovely Frau Dagmar Hastrup with soft pink single flowers, the very popular Blanc Double de Coubert which has papery white flowers, and Pink Grootendorst with its rose-pink frilled flowers that I find so attractive and which, like all rugosas, flowers throughout the summer, if rather patchily. Another plus is their marvellous hips in autumn.

There are some near-wild roses which are definitely worth growing. For instance R. *rubrifolia*'s charming light pink flowers do not last for long. But the deep purplish-red foliage remains very striking and come autumn the hips are glowing. Canary Bird also flowers for a short time, but its arches of wonderfully vivid yellow tiny open flowers will take your breath away.

The Bourbons include some magnificent roses, such as Souvenir de la Malmaison whose many petals start at the outside as white and become blushed in the centre. Faced with a perfect-looking example I swear you will name it your favourite rose. Mme Pierre Oger has a very soft blush and is really dainty. Then the Bourbon which is so much grown for its brilliant rich pink flowers and its wonderfully thornless branches is Zéphirine Drouhin. I have the climbing version of this. It flowers early and never fails to cause a stir when it does.

In reality there is not a strict distinction between what people call old-fashioned roses and modern ones. For some of the oldest-looking roses like Nevada were in fact introduced in 1927. My other great favourites – the hybrid musks such as fine light pink Penelope and Felicia and soft apricot Buff Beauty are the fruits of the breeding programme of an English clergyman, the Reverend Joseph Pemberton, in the 1920s. Before the invention of the floribunda, hybrid musks were used a good deal for bedding and I still grow a good number for their sheer beauty. They do flower in summer and in autumn but with none of the persistence of a floribunda.

Other totally delightful 'musts' for your border are little polyantha roses. These are a variety which produce many hundreds of tiny flowers on one stem. In fact some modern polyanthas like Yesterday – which is a lilac pink rose of great charm – can grow to sizeable bushes about three feet tall. A pink version which particularly catches my eye is Ballerina. I grow both of these in an herbaceous border, mixing them in among the flowers, and they look so natural and charming. I have also seen them grown very effectively as standard roses.

Standard roses can look wonderful. They can also look ghastly, when planted in a line in front of the suburban home with nothing behind them as softening backdrop – just a row of surprised-looking bushes on three-foot stakes. But a visit to one of the divine French rose gardens outside Paris, such as Roserie de L'Hay-les-Roses, Avenue Larrounes, 92240, will show you how they can be used. There they are placed formally at eye-catching intervals between the romantic arches of ramblers such as Wedding Day, New Dawn and Dorothy Perkins. They are generally weeping standards with their branches covered with thousands of tiny noisette roses – Excelsa, Albéric Barbier, Thalia are among those you will find – and these appear so much more natural than the upward-looking, hybrid tea standard so common in England. However, if you get a standard of Yesterday or Albéric Barbier and mix it in the herbaceous border with delphiniums and verbascums reaching up around, and shrubs behind it, I can guarantee that you will find the effect ravishing.

White gardens

Certain plants, like certain women, tend to look their best after sunset. And it is well known that the flowers that really come into their own in the evening are the white ones which suddenly stand out as the surrounding colours fade. By coincidence, it is often these white flowers which give out the best scents. At this time of year the garden becomes for most of us the most important room in the house. We eat in it, on balmy nights I sleep in it, and we relax in it after hot days in the office drinking in the heady and calming smells. So the area where you choose to sit in the evening – generally the spot which gets the last sun – requires a lot of thought. It should look enchanting and smell divine.

A friend I visited once in France had given over his 'evening garden' (the west-facing side of the house) entirely to white flowers and shrubs. *Clematis* Henryi, *C.* Marie Boisselot and *C. balearica* climbed up the *Hydrangea petiolaris* and the rose Mrs Honey Dyson. Meanwhile a rose called *filipes* Kiftsgate (which grows many feet a year and should only be grown up the sturdiest of trees) was making great headway up an old tree. *Wisteria sinensis alba* clung to the wall.

His shrubs were *Choisya ternata* (the white, glorious smelling Mexican orange blossom with marvellous glossy evergreen leaves) and *Deutzia setchuenensis* which produces hundreds of small white flowers from June to August but needs a sheltered spot to survive in England. Then there was a mass of white agapanthus, iris and nicotiana interspersed with gypsophila and anemones. Altogether a thrilling sight.

Few of us can think on quite that scale. Just now the white Regale lilies are a great addition to an evening garden. The other really strong smells are the white sweet peas – I can never get enough sweet peas and train them up everything including the apple trees – and the white tobacco plants (nicotiana). Coloured nicotiana has a less powerful scent. Other wonderful smelling climbers are of course honeysuckle and white jasmine.

Finally, it's worth investing quite a bit on lighting. My friend in France had the most subtle effects ranged out under shrubs and spotlighting climbers, so that after dark the garden became a fairyland.

Cover your earth

No doubt there is a word for it, but in high summer I suffer from a condition whose symptoms are an aversion to the sight of bare soil and a determination to obliterate it. Plants which provide ground cover will provide the double service both of keeping weeds at bay, thus saving you time and backache, and of preventing moisture from evaporating which means less watering. Above all, a really well-filled border, with variously shaped shrubs and perennials spilling over into each other, can be one of the finest sights you could wish to see – and a uniquely British one at that.

Ideally the time to put in your ground cover plants is from early autumn onwards. If you are going to do this now is the time to do your homework. For only by looking in other people's gardens can you decide what would look right in yours. Remember that some of the plants recommended in books are meant to cover large areas, and in most London gardens would run amok.

Ground cover plants should look appealing for a large part of the year. So when planning your border edge mix evergreens along with the perennials like geraniums which will die back in winter. Some of the prettier ones have fine colouring when not in flower, particularly the silver-leafed and variegated plants.

Of these silver friends I plant liberally *Hebe* Pagei; it forms a low-lying silver-blue clump which looks delightful all year round and then, as a plus, produces delicate white flowers in summer. Feathery silver *Anthemis cupaniana* also spreads in charming soft clumps and once your stachys, with its velvety leaves often called lambs' ears, gets going you will be pushed to stop it. Like all silver plants, a patch of this sets off other border colours so well.

Another silver gem is *Convolvulus cneorum*, whose white trumpet flowers bloom on for months, but this needs a sheltered sunny spot.

My number one favourite at present is *Alchemilla mollis*. I have often seen this in hedgerows and knew it as lady's mantle. I saw the breathtaking sight of a whole long pathway at Borde Hill in Sussex lined entirely in a mass of this limey yellow feathery flower which positively frothed over. It forms fine clumps and will seed itself all over the place.

Ivies and periwinkles are a boon, particularly in shady areas, and variegated kinds are most striking. If you have quite a big shady area to cover try good old St John's wort (*Hypericum calycinum*). It will spread away rapidly and has the bonus of pleasant yellow flowers as well as fine green leaves. Another good carpeter for shade is lamium. Don't let it loose if you do not have a lot of space. But if you do, its charming silvery variegated leaves will make their way over large areas. Then in spring out come the flowers, which look rather like a yellow or pink version of white deadnettle. Hostas will also find total happiness in a shady nook. With their great sculpted leaves in a wide variety of forms, from the green leaves and white margins of *Hosta decorata* and *H. crispula* and the many forms of *H. fortunei* to the yellow-leaved ones and the amazing grey-blue *H. sieboldiana*, they are quite the most classy and elegant of plants.

Out in the sunlight your helianthemums (rock roses) will form ravishing great clumps. So will many herbs like yellow marjoram which covers large areas and remains yellow all summer. Pretty little *Geranium endressii* will fill areas in your border between the roses, shrubs and more ostentatious plants and will cheer you up with its charming sugar-pink flowers all summer. It looks very fetching by blue or white spreading campanulas, such as lavender-blue *C. poscharskyana*, which are catching my eye this month – spreading onto paths and over borders at such a rate that no weed has a chance.

Seeds of thyme

Has it every occurred to you, returning home from a spell away to be greeted by a six-inch-high lawn, that there might be alternatives to grass? Probably not, unless you decide to put the whole thing under York stone and have done with it. Of course there are few things more glorious than a really well-kept English lawn stretching into the distance, but if you lack for space, you might contemplate something new.

I was thinking of this one summer day when I ventured down to Ealing to view a thyme lawn in bloom. I walked through an identikit red brick London house to find myself in an enchanting cottage garden. A large and splendidly shaped apple tree dominated all, while old-fashioned roses and honeysuckle climbed over the boundary fences and the flowerbeds were bright with foxgloves, columbines, white campanulas, candytuft and cottage pinks. And there in the middle was this haze of gentle purple: the thyme lawn.

My hostess seemed to have come by her thyme lawn almost by chance (this applied to her garden in general; the flowers all being the results of odd seed pods she had picked up). Someone had given her a clump, it had spread and over a period of ten years or so she had been dividing it up and replanting until it now spread over an area about fifteen feet by ten feet. Then – in July – it looked spectacular. The owners chose not to walk on it for the three weeks it bloomed both because they would hurt the flowers and because it became alive with bees – the cat had received a nasty sting the previous year. However, for the rest of the year you can walk on it happily – take your shoes off and it feels delightfully springy between your toes – and of course it needs no mowing. But you should watch out for weeds and be sure it is well watered in time of drought.

Of course thyme is not the only alternative to grass. My other favourite which is equally fine to smell is camomile – ladies used to walk on camomile lawns to get the nasty smells of the street off the bottom of their gowns.

You should wait until autumn to plant either sort and – as when sowing a grass lawn – it's important to prepare your patch first by flattening it and then raking in some humus material like rotted manure or peat. The camomile advised for lawns is *Anthemis nobilis* Treneague. With thyme you have a wide choice of creeping thymes (*Thymus serpyllum*) in various colours and you can indeed mix them as in the famous thyme lawn at Sissinghurst where various shades of purple, mauve, pink and white intermingle like a Persian carpet.

Take cuttings

Wandering around a particularly pretty garden open to the public I turned a corner and chanced on two magnificent ladies of the flowered hat and WI species admiring the border – or so I thought. Imagine my surprise to find that they were stealing. Plainly it did not come naturally; the lady keeping *cave* looked highly flustered while her friend – deep in the shrubbery – was very hot and bothered indeed. Taking cuttings from other people's gardens is a widespread crime indulged in by stalwarts who would in normal circumstances never step an inch the other side of the law. And surely you have felt the temptation yourself? Not only do you get a shrub for free, but – more important – many of the rarer shrubs just can't be found in your local garden centre. I have scoured the country for a particular camellia I fell in love with at Wisley. If I don't track it down in a catalogue soon, no doubt I shall also be caught red-handed.

If you are honest, however, and restrict your picking to friends' gardens, taking cuttings is rewarding and can positively cement your friendship. Every year I start up a few more shrubs in this way. I gained an oleander with little difficulty and also a lovely variegated *Euonymus fortunei*. For beginners nothing takes more easily than *Senecio greyi*, that useful silver shrub.

What is a cutting? In the words of Noel Prockter, a cutting is 'any portion of stem, leaf or root, separated from a plant but prepared and treated in such a manner that it can grow into a new plant'. With shrubs the simple way to start is with stem cuttings and now, when they are putting on lots of growth, is a good time to begin, though you can keep at it through the autumn.

To take a stem cutting, first ensure that the parent shrub looks healthy. Remove a side shoot (say six inches long) off the main stem and trim the heel with a sharp knife. Cut off the lower leaves for two inches. Make several cuttings this way, then plant them at a slight angle round a plant pot in narrow holes two inches deep (or a third of the length of the cutting) made by a stake or pencil. Firm the compost round them and water gently. Cutting compost should be half rough sand and half peat or compost – the important ingredient

Shrub cuttings (the example here is *Senecio greyi*). Pull or cut off a young but sturdy side shoot. Nip out the growing tip and remove the bottom few leaves on the stem.

being the sand which the tiny roots can cling to. It should be firmly packed down before making the holes and inserting the cuttings. Nowadays you can buy special rooting powders in which to dip the end of your cutting before planting. This gives them a head start, though a small dusting is quite enough.

At this delicate stage provide all the protection you can. If you have a propagator, that is ideal. But if not, a polythene bag popped over the pot and staked so as not to touch the cuttings should provide baby greenhouse conditions. Some people use jam jars. Some plants take much longer to root than others – *Elaeagnus pungens*, for example. But once the cutting is clearly making new growth you know all is going well. It is still very tender. Don't use fertilizer and keep it protected in a warm, even temperature. It should then be hardened off in a cold frame (or on a cool window sill) over winter to be planted out next year.

If you have space you should set aside a comparatively shaded, cool area in the garden as a cuttings bed. Shrubs such as hebe and buddleia, hydrangeas, spiraea, deutzia, euonymus and cistus should all take quite easily in this, or in a cold frame. Others require the more careful pot and polythene bag treatment.

Propagate geraniums

Other obvious plants to propagate now are geraniums or pelargoniums. These are all producing lots of growth and can spare a few side shoots.

Taking pelargonium cuttings just couldn't be easier or more satisfying, and once you've discovered the secret you will only buy new ones to increase your varieties. One June I bought the exquisite *P.* Lord Bute at Sissinghurst. This has deep wine-red velvety flowers which look particularly fine with white petunias. The next year there were scores of baby Butes. I was lucky to buy it. So many of the more unusual varieties are difficult to track down in shops, which is why in high summer many of us become dangerous predators in other people's gardens – no harm if you do a swap. Much the easiest plants to raise are the fleshy sort. So the *P. domesticum*, which comes in every possible shade of pink, white, red and mauve is ideal. The hanging ivy-leafed *P. peltatum* which I especially like is more of a challenge but generally does well. Of these La France – a very feminine soft pinky-mauve – is a timeless favourite.

Take cuttings of side shoots three to four inches long, removing the bottom few leaves and any flowers. Plant about an inch deep placing several cuttings in one pot in either a mixture of peat and sand or special cutting compost which has already been firmed down and in which holes have been made for the cuttings with a dibber or pencil. Make the cuttings firm, water them and then cover them with a polythene bag firmly held in place with an elastic band round the pot; and remember to keep them out of strong sunlight.

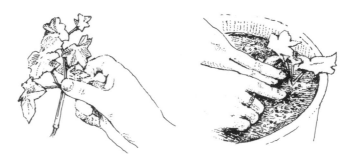

Pelargonium cuttings – use the soft-stemmed section of the plant. Insert a third of the stem into your potting compost which has coarse sand mixed in.

You can of course use trays with propagator lids; these will hold many more cuttings. The snag here is that if one cutting turns nasty – developing a vivid mould as one invariably will – it has more neighbours to infect. Yoghurt pots with a couple of holes in the bottom (which could take two cuttings) are as good as anything.

Water the cuttings from below if they look like drying out, but they should need very little and must never be allowed to get waterlogged. Within a month or two it will become clear from their healthy growth which cuttings have taken and become little plants. You can then remove the polythene along with any failures and in due course transplant to single pots. Don't expect total success, so always take more cuttings than you think you will need.

Sowing winter vegetables

If visiting flower gardens can be instructive, visiting your local allotments can be even more so. At this time of year allotments are all abuzz as the keen tenants pick and dig the fruits of their spring sowings and get going on the next. I have always found the atmosphere on an English allotment site so reassuring. Gardening brings out our best qualities. Everyone is happy to help you with a tip or tell you what he is up to. One allotment-holding friend told me that to him allotment life was a model of the ideal society: co-operative, competitive and classless.

The ingenious vegetable gardener rarely has a patch of earth in which nothing grows. Once you have pulled up those potatoes or carrots you can do a bit of catch-cropping – or fit in some sowings which will feed you in the autumn and winter. Good things to sow now are winter cabbages which you can continue to sow at intervals through until mid-August. You can do this in a seed bed, from which you have just planted out your leek, cauliflower and sprout plants, and plant them out in September or October which is more economical in terms of space. Or you can sow directly where they are to crop. Years of school food put me off cabbage; but not for good. A fresh cabbage, slightly under-cooked with a knob of butter is a wonderful thing. The Savoy cabbages such as Ice Queen, Savoy King and Best of All are very good bets.

The vegetable I can't have enough of is lettuce. You can keep growing summer-eating ones like Tom Thumb and Salad Bowl right though to the end of this month; but sow where they are to crop, as seeds planted now and then transplanted are likely to bolt. Come August you can start sowing the winter lettuces which you will relish so much as prices soar in the shops. The two really hardy standbys are Arctic King and Valdor.

There are many winter spinach varieties which if sown now will be welcome from November on. Try Long-standing Prickly or Sigmaleaf. Then of course there is always space for radishes. They grow so fast and will never fail to give your salad extra zest. Keep sowing small amounts until the end of next month and you won't be disappointed.

AUGUST

FLOWERS AND SHRUBS
Water plants copiously. Keep
deadheading annuals, perennials and roses. Continue
taking shrub cuttings. Take heather cuttings. Dry
flowers for winter decoration. Give liquid fertilizer
regularly to tubs, window boxes and hanging baskets.
Prune back old flowering shoots of rambler roses to base,
and train young ones. Plant out seedlings of perennials
like delphiniums, and biennials like wallflowers in a
special bed. Order spring bulbs by post. Continue spraying roses against mildew and pests. Take cuttings of
alpines like pinks and helianthemums. Prune shrubs
when they finish flowering.

VEGETABLES, FRUIT AND HERBS
Towards the end of the month plant new strawberry
plants. Keeping sowing winter lettuce, radishes,
cabbages (Savoys), spinach, beet. Sow onions
in seed bed. Transplant winter cabbage seedlings. After the fourth truss has set on outdoor tomatoes, stop the top. Cut down raspberry
canes that have finished fruiting to ground level. Tie new
canes to supports. Collect herbs for freezing and drying.
Keep putting out slug pellets. Increase herbs by taking
cuttings of sage, rosemary, lavender, origano, bay and rue.

PLANTS UNDER PROTECTION
Arrange for neighbours to care for greenhouse and house-
plants while you are away. Keep watering and feeding house-plants
and tomatoes, cucumbers and peppers. Spray regularly against
whitefly and red spider mite. Sow lily bulbils (from
the leaf axils of some lilies) in pots. Keep taking geranium
and pelargonium cuttings. Pot out young primula and
cineraria plants. Keep greenhouse ventilated and
shaded in heat.

OTHER JOBS
See the compost heap does not dry out. Apply
fertilizer on site of new lawn to be grown
next month. Keep mowing
regularly.

The constant rose

WHEN FLAMING JUNE is with us and even July, I sometimes find myself being a mite snooty about the modern roses – the floribundas and hybrid teas. For then it is the old-fashioned roses like the *Rosa alba* – Shakespeare's 'Pale and maiden blossom' which was the white rose of York – which steal the show for me. But from August through to October I make my apologies to lovely Lilli Marlene, Iceberg and Queen Elizabeth for previous neglect. For come what may these floribundas will flower on, always surprising you with their constancy.

It is a grave mistake not to plant some modern roses in a small town garden – these will see you through the summer and tend to be more compact than the old ones. Don't plant them in a bed all on their own, but mix them in among the shrubs and other flowers. They will look much prettier when flowering and when they die their rather sad, dormant shapes will not stand out bleakly to remind you it is winter. Lavender is a good mixer, as are other silvery bushes like santolina. Think in terms of grouping one variety of rose alongside a group of another, rather than going for a rainbow effect.

With hybrid teas people do tend to go for the brighter colours such as the vivid coppery orange of Just Joey, which really is very striking. Another marvellously vivid one is Alexander which its breeder Jack Harkness described as a 'luminous orange vermilion . . . a red rose trying to outdo an orange nasturtium'. A very new and simply lovely hybrid tea is Silver Jubilee which Alec Cocker introduced to the excited rose world in 1977, the year of his death. It is a rare, vivid peaches-and-cream colour and flowers so well that it is already popular. Another hybrid, Blessings, blooms a vivid pink and in abundance, and Mischief will bloom very freely, bearing many pink flowers tinged with coral.

If, like me, you go for the softer shades, the whites, gentle pinks and cloudy yellows, then of course you cannot ignore Peace. This heavenly rose is a soft yellow gently touched with pink. It is the most famous rose in the world. Its history – bred and nurtured in time of war by the Meilland family and then introduced to the world afterwards as a symbol of hope – is in itself as deeply moving as the flower. It is very common now but none the less high-class for that.

Other gentler hybrid teas are Pascali, with many fine white blooms, and the heavenly Elizabeth Harkness which is a soft ivory and buff colour with a tinge of pink. Ophelia is one of the oldest hybrid teas you can buy. It is almost white with a touch of yellow, a really elegant shape and a lovely scent. Michèle Meilland has a rather small flower, but the shape will really excite you. Again it is a soft shade of pink and therefore something that I would choose for my own garden.

The modern roses I most enjoy, though, are the floribundas. I grow a group of white Iceberg around the little statue of an eastern goddess in my garden. There is hardly a day from June to October that the bushes do not have at least a flower or two and sometimes they come all in a rush. At evening they are marvellously luminous and I also find they do quite well in dappled shade. Lilli Marlene is my other stalwart. In total contrast to the white Iceberg it is a deep, rich crimson which really stands out but is in no way garish. Everybody loves this rose and I find those semi-open blooms all clustered together in which you can just see the yellow centre very touching. It has a daughter called Marlena – from a match with Gertrude Westphal – which is brighter, rather smaller and also very lovely.

For the back of your border I can also commend Queen Elizabeth. This hugely tall, sugar-pink rose is often grown as a hedge. But it looks so much better vying with the hollyhocks and delphiniums in a border. It was in my first London garden when I arrived – along with some deeply boring hybrid teas which were given the push – and I left it there. For years it cheered me and provided endless flowers for the house. Meanwhile twelve years on it is still cheering my successors.

There are such a host of floribundas from the wonderful orange of Southampton, the open yellow of Saga and cheerful yellow Allgold that to choose for next year you should really go visiting gardens now and later in the autumn to see for yourself. But my newest favourite which I highly recommend is dear Margaret Merril. It has a soft white bloom of a really perfect shape, rather closer to a hybrid tea, and there is a subtle blush of pink in those clusters of flowers. But the punchline is to come: take a sniff and the smell will thrill you. She is a real knockout.

Cultivating neighbours

Nothing puts such a damper on holiday fun as the thought that back home your plants are pining. As the season arrives, so does the vexed question: who will tend your garden/house-plants/window box with such loving care that you can gambol with the kids at Frinton or sun with your love on the Costa Brava without a flicker of doubt in your mind. It's a responsibility not to be discharged or taken on lightly. Many a good friendship has foundered that way. I barely spoke to my sister for some time after she let a shrub perish in its tub.

The best solution is to find a gardening friend who holidays at a different time. That way you make a reciprocal arrangement in which both sides have a vested interest. Greenhouses in high summer need a daily water, the lawn must have at least one mow a week and the vegetable patch needs a regular water if the rains hold off. If you risk a non-gardening friend, remember that they will have absolutely no idea how much water plants need. I leave very strict instructions detailing exactly how long it takes me to hose the garden. If it hasn't taken them 20 minutes they are falling short. This is vital with a patio garden as tubs can dry out in a matter of days. Window boxes of course need water whether it rains or not – a fact of which those who don't own window boxes are unaware.

If you don't entrust your garden to another you should take certain precautions: mow the lawn last thing before leaving; have a good weed; give the beds a mammoth soaking before you go and mulch everywhere you can. The latter means covering every visible patch of earth after it is well and truly soaked with something to keep the moisture in. It can be compost or peat (I empty last year's gro-bags), grass clippings or straw, or rotted manure which I use on the tubs to give the flowers an added fillip. Finally, put moveable tubs in the shadiest corner to reduce the chances of them drying out.

In the greenhouse, keep ventilation going and use a lot of shading. Various firms now make automatic watering systems for pot plants based on capillary matting – an absorbent material which remains saturated and upon which you sit your plants. You can get it at any garden centre; but a cheaper way out is to cover your bench surface with polythene, placing a length of capillary matting on it. Soak the matting and place the end in a big bucket of water to keep moisture flowing through regularly. Then sit your pots on it.

This principle – the bucket of water and absorbent material – can apply to pots large and small. One year I tried the shoe-lace technique: soak a thick shoe-lace in water, prod one end deep into your pot, trail the rest of the lace in a jam jar of water placed slightly higher and the water should keep feeding the plant. With larger pots, you need a thicker material. For a week away, you might safely put your pots on a wet towel in the bath, leaving a tap dripping gently.

While on your holiday you can look out for ideas for your own garden. For example, judging from the newspaper advertisements, half the country is flinging out home extensions and garden rooms made largely of glass. There is no reason why in such a lovely light, frost-free place you should not permanently grow bougainvillea, that vivid and ravishing climber with a mass of pink, white, yellow or purple bracts which we associate with Spain and the south of France; or you might prefer oleanders.

I now have quite a collection of oleander bushes picked up as cuttings during holidays. To bring a rooted plant into the country requires a special licence which is hardly worth the trouble when you can take cuttings. Oleanders come in many shades other than the sugar pink we know. On the Riviera, you see streets lined with standard oleander trees ranging from deep red through pink to soft salmony shades, then yellow and white. There is also a variety with interesting yellow variegated leaves.

In England they would not grow so tall nor survive a severe winter. I have overwintered some outside for several years but in cold spells I trundled the tubs indoors to escape the severest cold. Always wash your hands after handling oleanders as they are very poisonous.

Fitting in the strawberries

Towards the end of July I begin to think I cannot look at another strawberry. Those great big mass-produced ones in the shops have none of the taste and subtlety of the smaller, more delicious ones you can grow yourself. So if you are thinking of growing strawberries and have the space for a bed, think carefully about the sort you will grow. You might put little alpine strawberry plants in your border, as I do, to seed and bloom and provide delicious little nuggets of taste in drinks. But to plan more seriously, you should write up for a catalogue (see Appendix VI) and plan to grow the varieties of fruit which will crop at a time when the shops are not awash with fruit themselves. There are, after all, strawberries which will crop in April.

Now is the time to plant all kinds of strawberries if you want a good crop for next summer. Plants are just arriving in the nurseries or you can get them by post from specialists whose deliveries take around two weeks. There are more than forty varieties on the market, but your nursery will probably stock about eight varieties, well tried for resistance to disease and variety of taste, size and season.

If you have very little space – or, perhaps, only a balcony – you can have great fun growing strawberries in pots. There are now those rather bizarre looking tower pots which are demonstrated every year at the Chelsea Flower Show with literally pounds of strawberries dripping from the lips and placed at intervals down the cylindrical plastic tower. I have tried these once without great success as I failed to feed and water them enough. But if you are prepared to be diligent, and can find a sunny spot for them, you can have excellent results. Another even more bizarre article is the Vertistraub. This is an amazingly ugly long dark polythene sausage which you hang up in your greenhouse. It is about eleven feet long and comes supplied with compost and twelve plants which you plant in holes in the polythene once you have stuffed your sausage. If you are lucky and look after it, it can produce thirty pounds of strawberries, so this really can be fun for someone without a vegetable patch.

The advantage of growing strawberries in tubs or tower pots is that you can take them indoors. Try planting Tamella, the spring cropper, in pots outdoors – strawberries need a cool period to form flowers. Come January bring them indoors to live on a sunny window sill and pray for your April crop. Or plant Gento, the late cropper, outside – these will provide delicious puddings in September when the shops have forgotten strawberries exist.

The well-tried wooden barrel makes a delightful container, particularly when painted white. Drill holes in the base, cut out plant holes twelve inches from the base and nine inches apart, put crocks for drainage in the bottom and then fill with potting compost (I use John Innes No 2 for all strawberry pots), placing the plants as you go up and then planting three at the top.

Remember that a strawberry plant is not much use after three years and so, nature being the good provider that she is, it throws out runners to create new plants. If you plant these in other pots you can have a good succession. The little runner takes about six weeks to root and then should be cut away from the parent and will fruit next year. One of the most delicious croppers of all is Royal Sovereign. It is not too big and not over prolific, but really worth growing.

Fraises des bois

I remember a friend saying that he discovered the secret extravagance of his bride-to-be when she ordered champagne with *fraises des bois* as a snack in Antibes. You too can make life seem luxurious by growing alpine strawberries from seed. Most seed companies stock them and they have the advantage of producing fruit for a long period during the summer. The true wild strawberry is *fraise des bois* which in France is often served as a luxury in restaurants.

The restaurant might in fact be serving you a heavier cropper like Alexandria which is a very sweet and juicy, large variety from Switzerland and which would do well in your garden. An autumn fruiting variety is Red Alpine. Sow the seeds in January or February, prick out the baby plants into boxes, then sow them outdoors in spring, nine inches apart. You should have a good crop the same summer.

Flowers indoors

Though Constance Spry was clearly a lady of high inspiration, I sometimes think she has also a lot to answer for. Pass any florist shop and you'll see what I mean. Spikey salmon gladioli perched in pyramid formation with dyed carnations on some plastic dolphin in a sub-Spry 'arrangement' which bears as much relation to the garden as those plastic roses which used to come free with the Daz pack. Enough to make Mrs Spry turn in her grave. Granted, the florists are limited by their materials. Commercial growers create long, straight-stemmed flowers for easy packing which make for the spikey look. The ideal solution is to grow your own.

As a child in the country our house was always filled with flowers: bowls of roses and sweet peas gave out heady smells and my mother would make brilliant arrangements including wild and wonderful hedgerow plants like old man's beard and corn. At the back of the vegetable garden was an area of flowers set aside just for picking. We town gardeners have neither the luxury of that space nor the hedgerows to glean. But we can make a start by growing certain flowers and shrubs which are particularly good both in the garden and for arrangements and which perhaps combine well with the bunch of chrysanthemums bought at the corner shop.

Once I had the fun of arranging the church flowers for a friend's wedding. In the large arrangements we used marvellous variegated elder called *Sambucus nigra* Aureomarginata which grows very tall and must be cut back ruthlessly every year. *Eleagnus fulgens* with its grey leaves and silver undersides is magnificent in arrangements and lasts weeks. Other silver foliage was *Senecio greyi* and various artemisias. We also used *Choisya ternata*, a lovely glossy-leaved evergreen which again lasts well, and *Berberus vulgaris* Atropurpurea, that long-stemmed purple-leaved shrub with surprising yellow flowers.

I attended a flower arranging demonstration by the famous Sheila Macqueen who quite took my breath away with her loose, effortless arrangements based on lady's mantle – *Alchemilla mollis*. Alchemilla is one of the ten plants for arranging which this internationally acclaimed flower arranger says she would hate to live without. The others are euphorbias, hostas (with their differing variegated leaves), hellebores, bergenias, ivy, arum lilies, artichokes (for their huge silver leaves) sedum (never a favourite with me, but a great laster) and *Phytolacca americana*, which is prized for its fine seed heads.

Tips on arranging flowers

Some people have an almost irritating knack of always knowing how to solve your problems. I remember being sent a fine bunch of tulips one spring. Placed in a vase in my office they instantly drooped – and my spirits with them. My neighbour down the corridor – a real Miss Fix-It – was on to them in a flash: out came the sewing needle and with great precision she neatly speared each tulip through the neck just under the flower. The pin pricks were barely visible. And when I next looked up – so had the tulips. It is tips like this that really separate the pros from the fumblers. But there are certain very basic commonsense rules about cutting and arranging flowers and foliage which will keep the flowers fresher for days longer.

Nothing cheers a room more than a bowl of fresh flowers, and however small your garden there is no reason why you should not have flower arrangements throughout the summer. In a garden like mine one cuts the flowers very sparingly and occasionally buys a bunch of daisies to supplement. But I never lack for foliage, which makes up over half the arrangement. In summer, shrubs are putting on tremendous growth, so cutting for arrangements is just another good method of pruning.

An arrangement consisting of the deep glossy green *Viburnum tinus*, lovely variegated leaves, *Weigela florida* Variegata, some silver leaved *Senecio greyi*, some flowering purple hebe, a few twigs of copper-coloured *Berberis vulgaris* Atropurpurea and some sprigs of lavender does not need more than a handful of flowers to lift it to look quite special.

Always remember to cut flowers and foliage either in the early morning or the evening when it is cool. It is crucial not to seal off a flower's water supply, and there is less risk of this if you can pick with a bucket of tepid water in hand to plunge them straight into. Cut stems on the slant, so there is more access for water and in the case of thick stems slit them an inch up. Also remove the lower leaves which would otherwise decay, standing long in water. If a cut flower has been out of water for a time you must cut its stem again. If you do this, keeping the stem under water, there is less chance of its sealing up. Some flowers like spurges and poppies have stems which give out a milky substance. You can stop this running by lighting a match and singeing the cut end.

If, as sometimes happens in town, the evergreen foliage is dirty or dusty why not swish it around in a bucket of tepid water adding a small squirt of washing-up liquid? But remember to rinse afterwards. Plants also absorb water through their stems and leaves. And the more they get the longer they survive. To help this, professional flower arrangers will always immerse foliage in water (they use special deep buckets) overnight or at least for some hours. But be aware that young shoots can get waterlogged if left there for more than a couple of hours and silver leaves will lose their silver.

Another method of helping woody stems like branches of shrubs and roses to absorb water is by dipping their stems in boiling water one inch deep for a minute or so. For this you should set aside an old pan no longer used for cooking – or you risk poisoning the family. This method can also revive wilting flowers. Lastly, always consider your flowers' feelings and keep them cool. Nobody wants to sweat by the fire or on the TV or just sit stewing in the sunlight and neither do flowers.

Drying for winter

Throughout the winter the entrance hall in one of my friends'
houses is always welcoming and pretty. She may not have been able
to pick fresh flowers in January, but there is, each year, a new
entrancing arrangement of dried summer flowers . . . a memory of
warm evenings and a hint of better ones to come. A lot of the flowers
which form a crucial part of her annual arrangements are in bloom
now. Some, like those enchanting papery-red Chinese lanterns, the
Physalis franchetti, are grown specially as 'everlasting' flowers. But
others, like golden achillea and acanthus and the many grasses, are
just ordinary garden plants which happen to dry well.

So if you have a dark (light will fade the flowers), cool, but airy
place in the house, set it aside as your flower drying cupboard.
Flowers should be picked when they are at their peak of perfection.
If you cut them when they are not properly out they will probably
wilt. They should be tied loosely with raffia or string and hung in
little bundles upside-down to dry. Once they are clearly quite dry
remove any shrivelled leaves and then store them in boxes or set to
arranging them.

Some flowers that will dry well this way are helichrysum, the
straw flower, which comes in both bright and gentle colours, the
lovely paper-light *Limonium sinuatum* and its relation the sea
lavender, cornflower-like catananche and honesty (lunaria). Another
wonderful addition is *Eryngium maritimum* which is that great blue
thistle known as sea holly. Then, of course, there are those hosts of
ornamental grasses which give glorious shapes and are easy to dry.

Other really striking shapes are artichokes whose heads dry well,
acanthus whose strange almost evil-looking greeny-purple flowers
will turn a gentle yellow, and glove thistles or echinops. Hydrangeas,
which in life can display such uninteresting colours, turn the most
subtle shades in death. I always dry them. It goes without saying that
all kinds of heather will dry beautifully. Many people also preserve
poppy heads and seed pods of flowers like love-in-a-mist for their
interesting shapes.

Of course, no flower arrangement is complete without foliage.
Here again you can preserve. Make a mixture of one part glycerine
and two parts water. In this you can stand the stems of foliage such

as beech, eucalyptus, lime and hornbeam and preserve them that way. A lot of plants will preserve better with this method. I am told that hostas – those amazing plants grown largely for their wide and various leaves which are always a flower arranger's standby – will turn to pale yellow. I think it's worth experimenting with many of your favourite flowers as long as they seem quite sturdy. Come the long winter evenings, you can make your arrangements (plasticine is very useful for this) and have some delightful Christmas presents – if you can bear to give them away.

Saving seeds

Nothing in my garden gives me more pleasure than to find that my favourite flowers have seeded themselves. Suddenly, when I least expect it, pansies will pop up. I had the idea of growing sweet peas up my small apple trees; then, as if it had read my mind, one obligingly seeded itself and did just that. A notorious and welcome spreader is aquilegia, of which I can never have enough. I was thrilled to see that my one *Alchemilla mollis* plant bought for a large price has spawned some twenty little plants nearby. Of course you do not want all your garden flowers to go to seed. Nor do you want certain varieties to reproduce because, if they are F1 hybrids – which are created by a seedsman by crossing two strains of a particular breed – they will grow versions of their dowdy parents rather than their dazzling selves.

In fact the secret of keeping flowers like pansies, sweet peas, antirrhinums and petunias flowering vigorously throughout the summer, is to constantly remove their dead heads. At this time of year when I am not weeding, I am deadheading, so the plant's energy goes into making more flowers and not into creating seeds.

But if you want to collect the seeds of a particular strain to grow next year it is comparatively easy with many flowers. The indomitable Lawrence Hills, who from his position at the Henry Doubleday Research Association fights a lone but lively battle against the extinction of many of our older fruit and vegetable varieties, has written a booklet called *Save Your Own Seeds*. This concentrates on vegetable seeds, many of which, particularly lettuces, leeks, onions and spinach, are easily saved.

The important thing with all seeds is to keep them in a dry, dark place which is not too warm. Put them in envelopes rather than polythene bags or jars, for a live seed needs to breath or it will rot and die. With most seeds the rule is to wait until the seed pod is ripe and is just beginning to dry. At that point, you cut off the stem on which it grows, and hang it upside down in a dry place with newspaper underneath onto which the seeds will spill.

If you want to grow tomatoes from seed, don't use F1 and F2 hybrids and don't bother with a well-known variety like Moneymaker. Try a rarer breed. The best seed will come from fruit on the third or fourth trusses. Leave your selected healthy-looking tomato until it is very ripe. Cut the fruit open and scoop the seeds into a sieve, gently rubbing them between your fingertips under a little running water. Then lay them out on blotting paper and leave them to dry in a warm room. In about two days you can packet them up.

Roof gardens in town

The old East End of London, where the Commercial Road heads east, where the tower blocks rise and the juggernauts trundle by, is not a natural habitat for gardeners. So I was surprised when a certain Miss Hester Mallin wrote inviting me to view her garden. She had, she said 'a 23rd floor English country garden' and, having read my gardening column, thought I might be interested. And indeed I was. For Hester is a real Miss Greenfingers. Up there on her eight feet by ten feet patio, looking across towards Southwark and the river and braving sun and wind, everything seems to flourish. In August it was a blaze of annuals, perennials and roses. Petunias, snapdragons, varying shades of lobelia and cottage pinks, tobacco plants, salvia, fuchsia and alyssum all spring from scattered tubs and pots while up the walls grow sweet peas, runner beans, honeysuckle and clematis (deep blue President and pink Comtesse de Bouchaud). She loves sweet-smelling plants and while we sat in her tiny living room the combined fragrance of sweet peas, honeysuckle and tobacco plants wafted in.

Hester, who is 'strictly a slum child' born in West Stepney tenements a mere 200 yards away, started her garden in 1974. Since then she has invested an enormous amount of time and love but re-

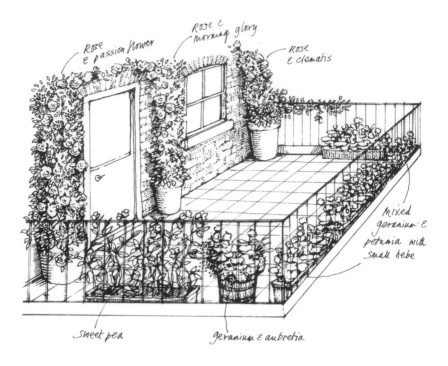

Rose & passion flower

Rose & morning glory

Rose & clematis

Mixed geranium & petunia with small hebe

Sweet pea

geranium & aubretia

Place tubs around the side of a balcony to reduce stress on the roof and give space to sit. Grow many climbers to cover the wall space.

markably little money in it. Most of the shrubs and roses were Woolworth throwouts at 25p a go which she has nursed back to health. The window boxes are either old plastic sausage boxes or polystyrene tubs which she painted up after having found them thrown out. They are ideally light so there is no stress on the roof. The climbers grow up plastic netting.

Many plants were taken from cuttings and she continually takes more to give away. When her shrubs and trees get too large and are beyond pruning back, she gives them to friends, so her plot is constantly changing. She hopes that her lovely slow-growing red Japanese maple will be faithful for longer.

Of course, plants do tend to flower profusely if their roots are constricted but only if they are fed and watered regularly. So a combination of small pots, regular watering and a regular dose of Phostrogen during the growing season from May ('I just wait for the garden to tell me it's ready') creates this riot of colour.

Hester is proud that her garden with its hundred or so different varieties looks good all the year round. In winter, evergreens and berries flourish. *Daphne odora* nuzzles winter jasmine, cotoneaster, camellias, bluish Skyrocket and the variegated leaves of elaeagnus, aucuba, Goldheart ivy and euonymus. Glossy-leaved mahonia is a new introduction.

When spring arrives, up come the bulbs which have remained in the tubs throughout the summer and are none the worse for that. She loves creamy white daffodils (Mount Hood), snowdrops, little blue chionodoxas and scillas, anemones in varying colours and rockery tulips. No garden is complete without something to eat. Strawberries apparently do nicely, as do redcurrants and raspberries. Little pots of sage, basil, mint, thyme and chives spring up at random. But her triumph is the parsley. It grows everywhere, pushing its vivid green leaves up among the petunias and geraniums.

Parsley can be a notoriously difficult herb to get going. There is an old story that before a parsley seed decides to germinate it asks the Devil what kind of person the gardener is, good or evil. If he is evil, the parsley goes on strike. If he is good it will flourish for him. As I left, Hester kindly gave me a bulging bag of parsley.

If you have a flat roof going to waste – perhaps on your kitchen extension if it is strong enough – take a tip from Hester. Large towns like London and Birmingham are full of them and could look so much greener if the residents or office dwellers used more imagination. Some roofs like Hester's get good sun. But those facing north and exposed to wind can also be made to bloom. A little sheltered roof garden leading off a first floor room can serve quite a different function and in summer become a genuine extra room.

I was reminded of this when a friend asked for my thoughts on a little roof leading off her flat. It was typical of many: quite small (thirteen feet by eight feet) with not much sun – being an extension roof it had a high wall behind and faced north-east so that even in high summer the sun disappeared smartly after lunch – and it had a noisy road running on the north-west side. Not ideal conditions for the combination of wild country garden and tranquil Alhambra that she had in mind.

When tackling this sort of problem, the first step is to give shelter, and cut out noise but not sun, by building a solid high fence on the north-west side. On the other two sides a two-and-a-half foot wire fence will do (unless you are very handy the Yellow Pages will find you a fencing specialist). Next, check what load your roof will bear. Large tubs filled with wet earth weigh a ton, and so should be kept only to the loadbearing areas. So long as you use good-sized tubs (say eighteen inches tall by twenty inches across), water and feed them very regularly with fertilizer and manure, there's little limit to what you can grow. Once I had a large roof garden and every autumn there would be a dreadful morning when, dressed as a dustman, I had to heave great sacks of horse manure up four flights to my roof. Throughout the summer I used liquid feeds and regularly raked fertilizer into the soil.

My friend wanted to concentrate on climbers and hanging baskets to keep floor space as free as possible. For the instant jungle she demanded I nervously advised polygonum – a climber which will cover the high fence in a year or two and is aptly called mile-a-minute. When the slower growers get moving it might have to go. Another ideal speedy climber is the honeysuckle *Lonicera japonica* Halliana. This is an evergreen, flowering continually and smelling divine.

There are a good many climbers which do not need full sun including many roses and clematis. I've grown Mermaid (a lovely single yellow rose flowering from June to October) and Alberic Barbier (a rambler with clusters of creamy white double flowers) successfully on a west wall. Mme Grégoire Staechelin (a large flowered climber with coral-pink blooms) can flourish on a north wall.

Clematis can climb gamely up the roses; C. Henryi (white) and C. Nelly Moser (pink and deep pink stripes) should both do well as should the *C. jackmanii* like Gipsy Queen (dark velvety purple) or Comtesse de Bouchaud (soft mauvy-pink). Most of these bloom in high summer. For an earlier display of tiny star-like blooms try C. *montana*, which grows apace.

Common white jasmine (*J. officinale*) is not much grown though it is quite excellent in tubs and romps along fences. It should have a fair amount of sun and will then produce hosts of tiny sweet-smelling white flowers. Annual climbers like sweet peas and *Cobaea scandens* will be a great addition particularly in the first year before the rest have made a spurt.

SEPTEMBER

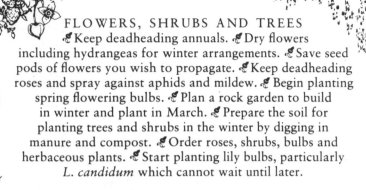

FLOWERS, SHRUBS AND TREES

Keep deadheading annuals. Dry flowers including hydrangeas for winter arrangements. Save seed pods of flowers you wish to propagate. Keep deadheading roses and spray against aphids and mildew. Begin planting spring flowering bulbs. Plan a rock garden to build in winter and plant in March. Prepare the soil for planting trees and shrubs in the winter by digging in manure and compost. Order roses, shrubs, bulbs and herbaceous plants. Start planting lily bulbs, particularly *L. candidum* which cannot wait until later.

FRUIT, VEGETABLES AND HERBS

Continue sowing winter cabbage, lettuce and spinach. Thin out earlier sowings. Start to order new fruit trees and bushes to plant in the winter. Prepare the site where you will plant fruit trees by digging in manure or compost. Continue to plant strawberries. Take cuttings of blackcurrant, gooseberry and redcurrant bushes. Cuttings should be about 9 in. of this year's wood. When blackberries, raspberries, loganberries etc. have fruited, cut the canes back and stake the new canes. Towards the end of the month pull up your tomato plants. Unripened fruit will ripen if put in a paper bag in a drawer.

PLANTS UNDER PROTECTION

Plant spring bulbs to force indoors. Sow sweet peas now or in October for early summer flowering. Reduce watering and feeding of house-plants. Continue taking shrub cuttings. Remove all plants from the greenhouse and wash it with Jeyes fluid, scrubbing benches. Close the windows and give it a smoke. Continue taking pelargonium cuttings. Also try impatiens and fuchsias.

OTHER JOBS

Keep weeding. Rake your lawn to rid it of dead grass and moss. Give it autumn lawn fertilizer and aerate it. Complete any maintenance jobs before the weather breaks. Feed fish in your pond.

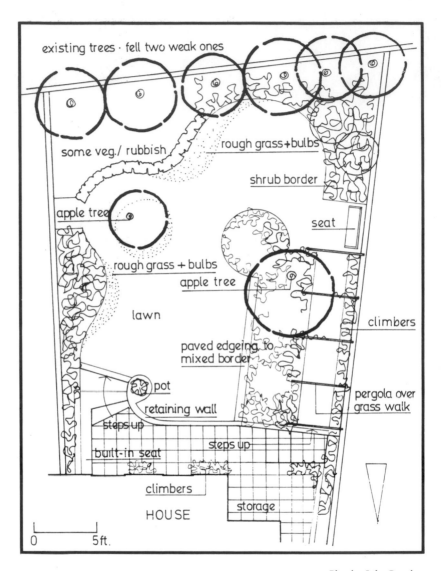

existing trees · fell two weak ones

some veg./ rubbish

rough grass+bulbs

shrub border

apple tree

seat

rough grass + bulbs

apple tree

climbers

lawn

paved edgeing to
mixed border

pot

retaining wall

pergola over
grass walk

steps up

built-in seat

steps up

climbers

storage

HOUSE

0   5ft.

Plan by John Brookes

Designing a garden

A TRUE GARDENER always has one eye open for ideas that can be adapted and used in his own little plot. Throughout the summer he diligently takes notes and only just about now begins to think of what could be made of that jumble written on the backs of envelopes. For September is the time when you can plan in a leisurely way. As far as the garden is concerned, summer is far from over. On the other hand, in a month or two you will be busy digging up new beds and planting new shrubs and plants. If you are planning a garden from scratch then this is quite the best time to start.

For a gardener, moving is not nearly so much a case of 'moving house' as of 'moving garden'. When I moved last, my new garden, covering an area thirty-five feet wide by fifty feet long, with mature lime trees at the back and two enchanting fruit trees in the main part, was almost entirely paved over with concrete slabs – giving it the look of a municipal playground. The first move was to bring in a garden designer, called John Brookes. Why, asked my friends, could I not do that myself? But I stuck to my guns. If you are building a new house you need an architect, though you may not need an interior designer. Similarly, I needed a real pro who after conferring with me could give the garden a structure. After that the planting schemes and all the fun would be mine.

And the structure I got was indeed much more radical than anything I would have dreamed up. For a start it involved bashing down a concrete retaining wall immediately outside the kitchen door where, before, you walked straight up steps onto the garden level about two and a half feet above. Then an area eight feet wide and the width of the house was to be dug to make a patio (this involved filling three skips with clay and rubble). Some of the concrete slabs which – being weathered – looked alright, were laid for the patio and then a pleasant brick retaining wall was planned with steps leading up to the garden on either side.

At the garden level all slabs were to be torn up and three borders planted: one each against the south-facing and the north-facing walls and one majestic one eight feet wide, divided by a little straight path from the south-facing border, which swept round under the pear tree and out into the centre of the garden. Then a lawn was planned: formal at the front but then becoming wilder with rough grass and bulbs at the back.

All this was done. Now you walk out of the house into a sheltered patio which is awash with potted plants – oleanders, bay trees, herbs of all sorts – and has comfortable elm seats. In summer I can eat out there with no commotion. Then a few steps up and you are in the garden proper, most of which is visible from below, but some of which – due to the craft of my designer's sweeping border – is hidden like a secret garden for you to discover as you wander down the path. I contemplated giving the plan to a contractor and letting him get on with it. But the quotation was so huge that I decided to employ people – the diggers and bricklayers, skip suppliers etc. – myself and did it for just about a third of the price quoted and with much greater satisfaction.

If you want to be bolder than I and do the plan yourself there are quite a few excellent books to guide you. The first thing is to get some graph paper so you can make your plan to scale. Then think about your needs. Most town gardens want the sitting area near the house with things like herbs for cooking within easy reach whatever the weather. However, you may want to also create a secret place at the bottom of the garden where members of the family seeking tranquillity may find some peace and quiet.

Perhaps you may wish for a small summer house to create a feature. You are bound to need a potting shed – hidden but near the house. Greenhouses are useful things but should not be given pride of place. Here again subtle screening is the key. I am a pergola fanatic. It is not that difficult to erect a wooden one – in my last garden which was long and thin I had a wooden one built from the house over the fifteen feet by ten feet sitting-area just outside the kitchen. You can then grow wonderful climbers over it. Or you might choose to build one shading the route to your secret garden.

Think long and hard about paving. York stone is expensive stuff, but it is a much nicer material for your patio than concrete slabs. Brickwork can look marvellous if you can get the old bricks; and if your garden is very much an extra room to the house you could use terra cotta tiles. I have London friends who have made a feature of the fact that their garden is entirely surrounded by high whitewashed walls and made the whole thing look as if you have been transported to southern Spain complete with the terra cotta tiles and tubs and masses of potted shrubs and flowers. Another charming paving is pebbles laid in concrete. The Greeks make an art of this forming wonderful mosaics in shades of white, grey and black. In a basement garden they can look particularly special.

But whatever you plan remember that every garden is different and while you can glean a lot from books your final scheme very much depends on the assets or defects you inherit. If you have a glorious view you want to make the most of it. If you have a wonderful old apple tree your plan should be made to emphasize it. If you face ugly walls you do your best to hide them. Don't feel you have to have a lawn. With children it is pretty essential, but otherwise paving with flowers growing up between the slabs and beds can be doubly attractive. For your own convenience put all your lawn area in one place – not a little bit here and there – or you will curse your scheme as you clip and mow till kingdom come.

Bulbs indoors

Planting spring bulbs should be a cheering thing. But I somehow get depressed when the first hyacinth and snowdrops bulbs make their debut in my local garden centre. For whatever the weather may say, it is a sure sign that summer is on the way out fast. Looked at another way, however, they are a wonderful antidote to winter gloom. Many people race to have bulbs flowering for Christmas and you should plant specially prepared bulbs early this month if you want that. But I prize them more in January and February when my spirits reach their lowest ebb and a sweet-smelling hyacinth in my bedroom or a bowl of daffodils in the sitting room can do wonders for low morale.

If you have a garden you should get into the habit of buying bulbs for indoors one year, with a view to planting them outdoors once they have flowered to come up the next year. For instance, you might buy thirty bulbs of a particularly prized narcissus from one of the specialist firms. These will go into two or three bowls of compost at fortnightly intervals to bloom indoors in February and March and will be flowering outdoors in March or April two years hence.

But to do this transferring trick it is sensible to use good soil or compost in a plant pot (this can sit in some pretty bowl to hide it). The bulb fibre which is often recommended, and is essential if you use shallow bowls with no drainage, contains no goodness and so the bulb will not build up resources for next year. Similarly those delightful glass bulb vases in which you place one hyacinth bulb and let its roots grow into the water, will do it no good for next year (though I love them as a way to show children how bulbs grow).

All hyacinths are good for indoor planting but I prefer the multi-flowering varieties which have several graceful spikes on one bulb. They look more delicate than the sturdy, one spike varieties and also more natural in the garden. Paper White narcissi are famous as indoor bulbs and have the advantage, unlike other narcissi, that they can be placed immediately in the window after planting. But most daffodils and narcissi will do well so long as they are not too tall.

There are two kinds of indoor spring bulbs: those that have been artificially prepared and those which have not. The first have undergone a process called vernalization whereby the nurseryman has kidded them – through manipulation of light and temperature – into thinking spring is nearer than it is. Some tulips and narcissi are prepared in this way. But the famous bulbs for forcing are hyacinths. For these, the rule of thumb is seventeen weeks from planting to flowering. So if you plant them now they'll flower in late January. Untreated bulbs take longer, giving you a succession of blooms.

You can plant hyacinths either in bowls or drained pots. If you choose bowls plant the bulbs shoulder to shoulder in bulb fibre leaving their tops showing, and moisten the fibre completely. In pots use John Innes No 1. They will then require a dark, cold period. Those in plant pots can be covered with peat, plunged in a flower bed and left for eight weeks in the case of prepared bulbs, and twelve weeks for ordinary ones.

Those in bowls would flood outside, so find your coldest spot indoors, and wrap them in thick damp newspaper. When the shoots are about one inch long bring them into a lighter cool place and, once the flower buds appear, into the light and warmth of your living room. The advantage of using plant pots and compost is that the bulbs get some food and can be expected to flower – though less dramatically – next year (fibre contains no food supply). My garden is full of old hyacinths which by now look like sturdy versions of their cousins the bluebells.

If you plant narcissi you can achieve a delightful effect by planting them in layers in a biggish plant pot. Put crocks in the bottom, some soil, then a row of bulbs, then half an inch of soil, another bulb row, more soil, a final row and about one inch of soil on top. This way you get more bulbs per pot and they grow at irregular heights which is prettier, I think.

Crocuses, particularly the large Dutch hybrids, look charming as do little pots of *Iris reticulata*, blue Muscari (grape hyacinths) or snowdrops which can then be transferred to a rockery. Do not try to mix up varieties. It sounds a nice idea, but the chances of them all blooming together are very slim indeed.

Grow love-in-idleness

Richard Cawthorne describes himself as a 'viola and violetta specialist' and when I came across his minute stand at the Chelsea Flower Show one May it quite took my breath away. All through the summer I thought about it, wishing that I had little clumps of lovely Laverna (a soft violet colour on a white ground) or Irish Molly (with its amazing sulphur and khaki markings) and a host of other violas and old-fashioned show pansies flowering continuously in my own garden.

I had already grown white and mauve *Viola cornuta* and had raised a pretty viola called Campanula Blue from seed (Dobies) so I know what delightful stalwarts they are, giving flowers from spring right through to November. Growing low, they are ideal for the front of a border, for rock gardens, or for window boxes, and they actually prefer a little shade so they can add colour to a north wall. They are also – unlike most modern pansies – very hardy. But Mr Cawthorne's collection was something else. I had never seen such enchanting colour combinations and such delicacy. No wonder that heartsease – which is ancestor of both the modern pansy and violas – was known by such nicknames as love-in-idleness, tickle-my-fancy and cuddle-me-to-you. I looked up violas and show pansies in many catalogues and found that very few nurseries stocked even a handful. Mr Cawthorne, who lists a hundred and thirteen varieties in his catalogue, is alone.

So one week in September I went to visit him. He raises his violas – over two hundred and fifty different varieties, many created by himself – on different patches of land around New Eltham. He took me to an allotment which he had transformed into a magic carpet of violas. But this was nothing, he said. They are at their peak in June and July when people come from far and wide to see them. I have never been a great fan of the more garish modern fancy pansy. But their ancestors the old-fashioned show pansies, many of which were bred in the early nineteenth century by Lord Gambier's gardener, a Mr Thomson of Iver in Buckinghamshire, are much more delicate and are utterly enchanting. Show pansies developed from crossing various varieties of heartsease, and in 1841 the Hammersmith Heartsease Society (would that it had survived) held its first pansy show.

Violas developed around 1860 from crossing show pansies with the species *Viola cornuta*. Mr Cawthorne showed me many other wild viola species that he stocks including delicate little fellows from Macedonia, the Pyrenees, Mount Olympus and North Devon, together with some cross-breeds (back home he showed me the fascinating process whereby he inserts pollen from one flower into another under a magnifying glass and then protects the pollinated flower from promiscuous bumble bees by putting a tealess teabag over its head).

I especially loved his creation Aspasia which has almost white top petals gradually changing to deep yellow lower ones, and her pure white sister Virginia. He also raised Letitia which is pale red and purple, and Lydia which is yellow and lavender. He stocks all the old favourites like Maggie Mott which is soft, silvery mauve; wonderful Lord Nelson, which is deep violet-blue with a striking yellow eye and Barbara which combines mauvey blue and soft sulphur yellow.

In September he takes cuttings for spring delivery and keeps them outdoors under frames in winter. A viola cutting takes at least six weeks to root. Take a little side or basal shoot of the plant, remove any buds and its lower leaves leaving two at the top. The cutting should be about two and a half inches long. Dip it in rooting powder and insert it in a firm compost using a dibber (Mr Cawthorne advises Levington's Universal which has sand added but you could add some yourself to another compost). The compost should be in a deep tray.

Now I grow a good many violas as edging plants and they always attract the eyes of my visitors. There is now even one called Felicity which, since I'm a true egotist, I grow. It is a soft mauve with even softer yellow markings which are strangely flecked. Mr Cawthorne has caught me up in his enthusiasm for these little plants which somehow manage to touch the heart. He has also made me feel that growing them is something of a mission. 'The pansies, violas and violettas of the world are not ours to dispose of as we please,' he writes in his catalogue. 'We must make it our duty to hold them in trust for other generations to follow.'

Sweet peas

Who'd envy a sweet pea? By rights they should reign over the choicest spot in the garden – looking and smelling as ravishing as they do – whereas more often than not you track them down to a row by the cabbage patch where they languish in regimental splendour ready for cutting. Though I think them lovely as cut flowers, my enthusiasm for sweet peas in the garden is boundless. I grow them up everything – the climbing roses, the apple trees.

For town dwellers they have every advantage. They are easy to cultivate (children love growing them), and they flower continuously, which is crucial in a small garden where you cannot afford to have drab patches. There are now the dwarf varieties: Bijou and Dobies' new Little Elf, which are ideal for cascading in a window box. One year my mother grew tall ones indoors with great success, training them up strings in a sunny bay window.

You can of course wait until spring to sow your seeds *in situ*. But that way you won't see flowers until high summer. If, however, you get sowing now (the first two weeks in October are the recommended time) you will have large plants to bed out in spring and with luck have flowers by early June. Planting now, it is advisable to have some kind of winter protection. Mine winter in a polythene greenhouse, but a cold frame or large cloche will do. Choose good compost like John Innes No 1 and plant the seeds half an inch deep either in individual pots (little peat pots are a good idea because you can transplant without disturbing the roots) or in a seed tray.

Having hard shells, the seeds sometimes germinate erratically. To ensure against this some people clip individual seed skins with a sharp knife – at the opposite end to the eye – or alternatively soak them in water for twelve hours before sowing.

[99]

When the little seedlings get to four inches tall you should nip out the growing tips so that they will grow in a bushy way rather than straight up. Plant them out in spring in a good well-manured soil and feed well with fertilizer. The better they are fed the longer and more magnificently they will flower.

There are so many varieties to choose from that it is difficult to advise. The Galaxy varieties are particularly long flowering and have many flowers per stem, though if you fancy yourself in the local flower show perhaps the longer stemmed varieties would suit better. I generally buy a large packet containing a selection which are individually packed so you know which colour you are sowing, as opposed to the more common mixed packets. It is also possible to buy old-fashioned sweet peas. These don't have the frilly petals and look more like pea flowers but they smell especially sweet.

Variegated shrubs

In both summer and winter coloured or variegated leaves will create enormous interest in your garden whether the shrub is flowering or not. There are so many fascinating variegated shrubs, both deciduous and evergreen which – particularly if you have not got a great deal of space to use – will give more value per square foot than their green relatives. Obviously you don't want to put the whole of the garden over to shrubs with striped leaves, but a few will really cheer it up.

By far the most famous and popular nowadays is the elaeagnus which is an essential feature of my garden and which – unlike many variegated shrubs – seems to thrive in shade, its glossy gold leaves acting like a shaft of sunlight on an otherwise rather dull part of the garden. Another extremely beautiful addition to any garden is euonymus. The *E. japonicus* Ovatus Aureus grows into a large evergreen shrub and is justly popular with its golden variegated rounded leaves. However, my particular favourites are the *E. fortunei* which form smaller bushes, have more pointed leaves and are ideal for ground cover or spilling over the edge of a wall. I grow *E. fortunei* Gold Tip which has quite soft yellow markings. Silver Queen is more white while Emerald 'n' Gold is just what it says.

Most variegated shrubs will do better in sun and this is especially true of the golden colours – oddly the silver colours seem to mind less. For instance *Cornus alba* is a great addition to any garden. It is deciduous but in winter its red bark is very attractive. The Elegantissima variety has the most elegant pale green foliage prettily marked with creamy silver. I have it in a spot which does not get much sun but its markings remain vivid. However the Spaethii variety which is similar with golden markings, loses much of its beauty and becomes quite dull-looking in shade.

Another fine shrub which must have a lot of light to give of its best is the variegated weigela called W. *florida* Variegata. This is a really useful shrub. It looks charming well into the autumn and in addition has soft pink flowers in early summer. I also find that the leaves last wonderfully well in water and are thus a boon when arranging flowers.

If you want a bush which will really grow fast a buddleia – or butterfly bush – is a real ally. It will grow to a good size in a few years and after a while you will have to take pruning seriously, cutting it back hard in March. Its long clusters of flowers, generally in mauves, purples, or white, appear in late summer and give added pleasure because the butterflies love them so. The B. *davidii* Harlequin has also the bonus of being delightfully variegated.

There are several variegated forms of hebe, the most common and very rewarding being H. *x franciscana* Variegata which has creamy-edged green leaves and then produces the most charming soft lilac-coloured flowers. The snag, as with many hebes, is that it is not entirely hardy and a really cold winter can polish it off. However, I continue to grow them for their loveliness and also because they are ideal for tubs, since they put up with a lot of drought.

Only recently did I discover a really rather exciting addition to the variegated family, the variegated pyracantha called P. *coccinea* Harlequin. This has happily taken to a north-facing (though quite light) wall and cheers it up considerably. Another surprising one is the variegated form of *Cotoneaster horizontalis* which has the same white flowers and berries but has white-edged leaves which turn a soft reddish colour in autumn. It goes without saying that the hollies and ivies in their variegated form are tremendously useful (see December) and most of them, like the variegated vinca which I love so, also don't mind if they get landed in quite a shady spot.

Finally, I am particularly fond of the variegated pittosporums. Pittosporums are such interesting-looking plants anyway with that rippling edge to their oval leaves. They can come in soft green colours, copper colours and many with different kinds of variegation from grey-green with cream or white or yellow margins. At one Chelsea show the Somerset College of Agriculture put on a huge display of the many varieties, which only emphasized how few of them are easy to come by. *P. tenuifolium* comes in many variegated forms: Silver Queen, Variegatum and Garnettii to name but a few. If you chance on one, grab it. You may not have the opportunity again.

Making your basement bloom

The more I think about it the more surprised I am that the basement entrance has not been exploited more as an art form. For so many people in towns they are the nearest thing to a garden and on occasions when I have seen one that has been imaginatively cultivated it has been a really thrilling sight, despite the fact that it may only occupy an area twelve feet by four feet. To the right person, such restrictions present nothing short of a challenge. One year I planned just such a basement with a friend. By the time we had our plans laid out – and September is as good a time as any to do this – we had a mini-paradise to greet her friends as they arrived and no doubt to cheer the dustman.

The obvious problems in a basement are space and light. She was lucky in that hers faced south and the walls were painted a glossy white, which reflected light well so the plants didn't have to crane their necks to the sky. Floor space was tight – my first scheme would have totally blocked the dustman's route. But generally in basements there is one good-sized space – in her case to the right of the front door – where a large tub could sit. It is important that this tub should be wide (say about two feet) and pretty deep as this has to house all the climbers. After that it's a question of using your imagination as to what can hang from where.

There was just room for a small window box on the window sill, but we then lit upon the bright idea of attaching plastic window boxes to the bottom of the pavement railings, facing inwards. Of course plants in these would be prey to passing pickers, but they would always catch the eye of anyone looking out from the basement sitting room.

PLATE 5 SHRUBS.
From top left to right: *Hebe andersonii*; *Philadelphus coronarius aurea*; *Choisya ternata*; *Camellia* Donation; *Mahonia* Charity; *Elaeagnus pungens* Aureovariegata.

PLATE 6 FELICITY'S GARDEN BEFORE.

PLATE 7 FELICITY'S GARDEN AFTER.

PLATE 8 CLIMBERS.
From top left to right: Rose, Mme Grégoire Staechelin; Rose, New Dawn;
Ceanothus, Gloire de Versailles; *Humulus lupulus aureas*; *Clematis
orientalis*; Rose, Mermaid.

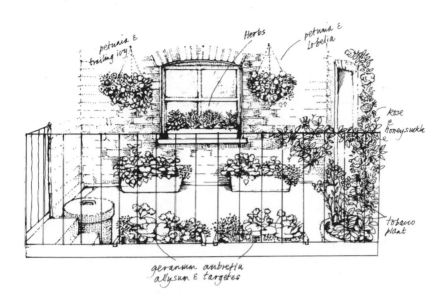

petunia &
trailing ivy

Herbs

petunia &
Lobelia

rose
&
honeysuckle

tobacco
plant

geranium aubrietia
allysum & targetes

Many basements seem to have an iron bar which crosses from the house wall to the street railings. My friend's basement was no exception; and this – with the landlord's permission – seemed an ideal hanger. We decided we would suspend a sizeable plastic tub from it, out of which ivy would drip in winter, to be joined by geraniums, petunias and other annuals in summer. Finally, two unobtrusive hooks could be put in either side of the window so that small hanging baskets of annuals could go up in summer.

For the climbers, I suggested a choice of roses. Mermaid is a good bet as it produces its lovely single primrose-yellow blooms throughout summer, and it doesn't mind a bit of shade. Nor does lovely shell-pink New Dawn which has the advantage of an enchanting apple scent. The Royal Horticultural Society's useful booklet *Plants for Shade* lists a wide selection of roses which flower in shade including the vivid orange-scarlet Danse du Feu and the blood-red Parkdirektor Riggers which both look very cheerful.

The roses could be trained over the doorway and up them you could climb a clematis. I recently saw a basement wall which was a blaze of purple *C. jackmanii*. (Avoid *C. montana*, by the way; it is too rampant.) Evergreen honeysuckle (*Lonicera japonica* Halliana) would be happy trained in the other direction. Alternatively you could try some variegated climbing ivy or Virginia creeper, or even a small vine. In the big tub you might put a shrub like a camellia or lovely white-flowered *Choisya ternata*.

The window boxes must look good all year. So, while leaving space to put in wallflowers next month, plant some little evergreen shrubs such as small hebes, which are very drought-resistant; *Senecio greyi* in a brighter spot; herbs like sage, rosemary and rue and perhaps some little conifers which spread. Trailing ivy always looks good, particularly the Goldheart variegated kind.

All the boxes and tubs should contain bulbs which can stay on from year to year. Baby daffodils, snowdrops, scilla and crocus will look really cheerful in spring and are coming into the shops now. They will overlap with the wallflowers (buy low-growing varieties) which will in turn be replaced by all manner of annuals (petunias, alyssum, snapdragons, French marigolds, the shorter tobacco plants, lobelia) come June.

Finally, remember to feed the soil. When planting this autumn add liberal amounts of long-lasting fertilizer like bonemeal. Every spring add more and then through the summer add a fortnightly tonic of liquid fertilizer.

OCTOBER

FLOWERS, SHRUBS AND TREES

Plant out wallflowers and forget-me-nots. Before flowers and shrubs fade, label those you want to move or divide as from next month (I use coloured ribbons). Prepare land where you are to plant trees and shrubs, digging in manure and compost. Clear beds of all annuals. Keep planting bulbs outdoors. Tulips should be in by the end of the month. Dig up dahlias and begonias and store tubers under cover. Cut stems of herbaceous plants and hardy fuchsias. Plant lily bulbs. If shrubs and trees are in moveable tubs, move them to the least exposed position.

VEGETABLES, FRUIT AND HERBS

Sow lettuces in seed bed, or frame. Plant out spring cabbage seedlings. Keep earthing up leeks. Destroy the stalks of Brussels sprouts and other brassicas. Double dig any new area you plan to sow in spring. Take cuttings of bush fruits; also prune them. Order new fruit trees and bushes. Put greasebands on large apple and cherry trees to stop attacks of winter moths. Take herb cuttings of lavender, bay and rue. Divide clumps of chives.

PLANTS UNDER PROTECTION

Bring pelargoniums indoors. Keep planting bulbs in pots or bowls. Disinfect seed boxes and stakes, and store for the spring. Plant some roots of mint indoors so you have it in winter. Pot up cuttings of geraniums and shrubs taken in July. Sow sweet peas in pots.

OTHER JOBS

Clear all fallen leaves off your lawn. Good time to lay a turf lawn. Stretch out a net to keep dead leaves off the pond and clear the bottom of muck.

Autumn glow

THIS IS THE SEASON when I find my garden most moving. Just when you feel it should all be over and the colours should be disappearing as the autumn mists set in, it starts its autumn fanfare. Those dreary pink hydrangeas turn a thrilling ruby/russet almost overnight and will stay that way for a good month before you pick and dry them for winter decoration.

Many other reddish tints appear as the leaves of bergenia, usually less politely known as Elephants' Ears, turn, in places, a vivid scarlet. (Bergenia should only be given a home if you have space and have a dry, shady area where little else can grow, where it is a boon.) Other red glories are the hips and berries which somehow glow more brightly in the cooler light. My old friend pyracantha is at its most brilliant now. So are many rose hips of the old shrub roses like rugosas. And we cannot miss the cotoneasters which are such a varied family ranging from the well-known *C. horizontalis* which is so useful for covering low walls, to the large *C. frigidus*, a Notcutts variety which grows to around ten feet with lovely crimson berries.

So many shrubs and trees are more interesting in berry than in flower. Pyracantha, being evergreen, is perfect for creating a tall thick neighbour-proof hedge. You can also get a yellow-berried variety such as *P. atalantioides* Aurea, and the white blossom in May is a bonus.

Among the most striking berried trees which I would like to grow and which look wonderful now are the mountain ash or rowan (sorbus) and the crab apples (malus). Many of the sorbus cultivated for gardens are Chinese varieties which come in a score of different hues, and grow more compactly than our native trees, eventually reaching a height of about fifteen feet.

Notcutts, who list twenty varieties in their catalogue, strongly recommend them for town gardens. *Sorbus aucuparia* Fructuluteo has clusters of berries the true orange of an orange fruit. *S. aucuparia* Fastigiata has wonderful red berries. But the *S.* Joseph Rock is more striking in that it produces primrose-yellow berries amid the green foliage which then turn to amber as the leaves develop their copper tints. For a change, you could choose *S. hupehensis* in its pink form which has the sweetest looking soft pink clusters of berries. All these trees have scented white flowers in early summer.

Of the crab apple family I wish I had room for *Malus* John Downie, whose vivid yellowish red, small apples look as if they have been polished, or M. Red Sentinel whose larger brilliant red fruits will last to March. M. John Downie is good for making jelly. A pair would pollinate each other, but a nearby apple tree would do. Both have pretty white flowers in spring. *Malus* Golden Hornet produces clusters of bright yellow fruit looking like so many bunches of golden cherries. I love it, as I also love the M. *hupehensis* with its profusion of little yellow-red berries.

Continuing the symphony of reds and pinks are the sedums, or ice plants. These sturdy plants forming clumps of succulent silvery leaves mind neither sun nor shade and are really useful for ground cover. The Autumn Joy variety produces lovely rosy-salmon blooms just now and entices the butterflies. *Sedum* Brilliant is a mauvy pink and I have a smaller, low-growing variety which is aptly named Ruby Glow. A specially exotic variety is S. *maximum* Atropurpurium which has deep copper leaves and stems and light pink flowers.

The other colour I associate specially with autumn is a sort of misty blue. This comes first from the agapanthus, which have now shot their bolt, and is taken up by the echinops, Michaelmas daisies and caryopteris. Echinops are those splendid blue thistles which again are excellent if dried for winter arrangement. I have a soft blue one called Taplow Blue. A smaller, more vivid one is E. *ritro*.

Caryopteris clandonensis is a comparatively new friend and one I have really come to love. It is a delicate silver-leafed shrubby plant which in mid-August comes into its very refined glory with many powdery blue flowers. They are quite wonderful in flower arrangements and striking in the garden. They can grow to about three feet tall and should be pruned right back to the base of their young growth in early spring. As mine are still flowering in October I consider them a real investment.

Autumn crocuses never cease to surprise me, associating crocuses as I do with spring. But they are in fact *colchium* and no relation to the more stocky spring bulbs. I love their elegant shapes and soft lavender colours which mix well with the other blues. The free flowering lilac C. *autumnale minor* and its white form C. *autumnale* Album are especially lovely.

Light does strange things to flowers and just now some annuals, particularly the tobacco plants, look quite different. In the greyer dusky light the white and lime-green varieties take on a quite new luminosity. I always feel particularly grateful to them and also to some sweet peas which I planted late here and there along an open north wall. They still flower now and will with luck keep at it until the first hard frost tolls the knell for all our lovely annuals.

Planting fruit

As everyone knows, autumn is the time to get planting. But it's not until the wind blows sharply, and you are reluctantly forced into winter woollies and that slow English drizzle begins that you really know the time has arrived. Just now my mind is very much on fruit, as I gather mulberries from a friend's dripping tree and thornless blackberries from the more modest plants in my garden. Meanwhile, the pears and apples are nearly there.

Few town gardeners have space or time to wait for a mulberry (they take many years to fruit but are very pretty as young trees) but all of us who can boast even a balcony do have room to grow fruit. Many soft fruits such as blackberries, boysenberries and logan-berries will romp away in tubs if given enough space and kept moist while raspberries, gooseberries, blackcurrants and redcurrants are better off having some area to themselves at the bottom of the garden where you can net them to protect from the birds. They are also not particularly pretty to look at. To help you choose which variety of soft fruit to buy, get hold of a catalogue (see Appendix VI) – they are always helpful.

Until recently I thought it wasteful to grow blackberries when there were so many in the hedgerows. But in fact a cultivated black-berry will produce much more fruit (try Himalayan Giant which can apparently yield twenty to thirty pounds of fruit per plant) and in some cases, for example Bedford Giant, will fruit as early as late July.

Much the prettier blackberry is the Oregon Thornless whose charming serrated leaves, which turn a reddish colour, would grace any wall. The fruit is delicious and if well nurtured each plant produces at least ten pounds of fruit. You might be more daring and try a blackberry hybrid like the loganberry which is traditionally said to be a cross between a blackberry and raspberry. They are beautiful climbers, ripening in July and August to produce huge wine-red fruit. Another hybrid is the boysenberry (supposedly a raspberry/blackberry/loganberry cross) which is darker, very delicious and again ripens in July to August.

When planting, remember that your bush will be there a long time so, as with raspberries, give it a good start – preparing the soil by forking in lots of rotted manure or compost. Himalayan or Bedford Giants, however, are good for poorer soils. Also, before planting, rig up a strong support system of wires along the appropriate wall. Otherwise you will regret it when the plants take off and become a mess of tangled canes.

When they have borne fruit, these climbers require an annual pruning. This should be done when the fruit is over and involves cutting back those branches on which the fruit grew right down to the base and training this year's new growth in its place to fruit next year. Redcurrants and gooseberries can also be grown against a wall as a cordon, which is a good spacesaver.

Finally, why not try an autumn fruiting raspberry? One interesting variety is Zeva which has the ability to fruit from July until November, its heaviest crop coming about now. Another one is Heritage which crops very heavily. Autumn fruiting raspberries are becoming nearly as popular as the summer ones, but they still have that lovely surprise element which makes anything appearing outside its traditional season a treat.

Hard fruit

It is at this time of year that I wish I had more room for fruit trees for not only do they give enormous satisfaction when the fruit develops, but their blossom is a joy in spring and I particularly like the rather knotty shapes of apple trees. Of course hard fruit (apples, pears, plums, etc. as opposed to soft fruit like raspberries and currants) need not be grown on single trees. You can get a fine crop against a wall if you grow cordons, which nowadays is what more and more people are doing. They use up less space and have the other advantage that you can ring the changes by growing, say, four varieties in a small area.

Sometime during the next four weeks is ideal for planting fruit trees and cordons. But you can continue to plant at any time until March if the weather is not frosty and the ground not waterlogged.

When planting, dig a hole large enough for the roots to spread out, but not so deep that the scion – the notch at the base of the trunk marking the point where the tree has been grafted onto a different, more sturdy, root stock – is covered by earth which could make it rot. Always remember to stake your tree or cordon firmly. Fruit trees need well-drained soil and should be staked to stop them rocking and sheltered to help the bees pollinate them. Ensure against fruit thieves by planting in the back garden.

It strikes me as silly to grow the likes of Cox's Orange Pippin and Granny Smith when at the time yours appear, the shops will be full of their perhaps more shapely cousins. Far more sensible to try a less well-known variety.

Another consideration is pollination. There is no sense in planting two neighbouring apples if they won't mate. I often find garden centre attendants remarkably unlearned on this crucial point. For when it comes to match-making, fruit trees are remarkably like humans. Instinct may tell you that two apples are just made for each other. You will plant them side by side and watch them blossom and think all is well. But they will stubbornly refuse to pollinate. So it's worth doing some homework before embarking on apple, pear or plum trees – apricot and peach trees pose fewer problems, being self-fertile.

You can plant throughout the winter, but November is the best time. Assuming your space is limited, and since most trees need a friend, you might co-operate with a neighbour by growing a tree each. A good catalogue should tell you which are likely mates. Bramley's Seedling (a cooker) goes well with many of the earlier varieties. Two late croppers, Edward VII (a cooker) and Crawley Beauty (dessert), will stretch your season until March and blossom later. Good pear mixtures are Beurre Hardy and Doyenne or Conference (which, again, is self-fertile) and William's. Plums are less tricky as many – including the lovely Victoria – are self-fertile.

Of course if your neighbours have apples there is a fair chance that their blossom will coincide and the bees will make it over the fence to cross-pollinate. If you want a thorough guide to the different flowering groups I find the Royal Horticultural Society's book *The Fruit Garden Displayed* (available from the R.H.S. at Vincent Square, S.W.1.) a cheap and useful reference. If your space is limited it is more sensible to grow eating apples (when you have cookers, so will everyone else). One good mix I could recommend is Epicure, an early fruiter, and Sunset which comes later.

If you really want to be different, try something that can give you two or three apple varieties from a space three feet square, solving your apple-mating problems at a stroke: the family tree. A family tree is quite literally a tree whose own branches have been removed when young (generally three years old) and replaced by grafting on several different varieties. Thus you may have a pear tree whose centre branch produces Williams flanked by Doyenne on one side-branch and Conference on the other.

The advantage is clear: not only do you get a good mixture in a tiny space, but also you don't have all your fruit arriving at once. For instance a three-branch tree could grow early Worcesters, Moss's Seedling and Laxton's Superb giving apples from August to February.

Family trees can be difficult to find, and for a good reason. All apple and pear trees sold in nurseries are grafted onto separate root stocks. Family trees go one stage further. You may have a perfectly saleable apple tree – say Discovery – which you must then deprive of its three-year-old branches, replacing them by others. With the demand for Discovery you might as well sell the tree and save the bother.

Matching breeds is also an art. They must not only be selected to cross-pollinate, but also to grow at the same pace so that the tree is well-balanced – a mature tree is about fourteen feet across. Some experts are sceptical of family trees, perhaps because the idea seems a bit unnatural and also because there is the risk with three different varieties that they will grow at different paces giving the tree an odd look.

Planting for spring

By rights I feel there should come a time when, with the exception of the odd annual, I need buy no more plants for the garden. The bulbs would blossom and multiply as would the herbaceous plants, and around this time of year I would divide them up so I could dot them further around the garden or give some to friends.

Take, for instance, polyanthus, that cheering spring plant with primrose-like flowers in all manner of gay colours on a stocky cowslip stem. Plant one now and after two years you will have the satisfaction of dividing it up into about five little plants thus starting the cycle again. And what could look prettier in spring than a border or bank of daffodils, bluebells and forget-me-nots with enchanting little primroses and polyanthus peeking through?

Before the month is out you should have steeled yourself to pull up your summer bedding even if your tobacco plants are still blazing away manfully – and consigned it to the compost heap or, in the case of tough-stemmed plants and rose clippings, a small bonfire. Geraniums should be put somewhere where they can withstand winter frost. Back in the garden your soil should be dug over, and given a good addition of compost or rotted manure to prepare it for the next inhabitants.

Polyanthus, forget-me-nots and wallflowers will give you bursts of wonderful colour from spring through to early summer when eventually you will have to pull out the wallflowers to make way for the summer bedding plants. They are all available in garden centres now and even your greengrocer will have boxes of mixed wallflowers. When selecting wallflowers bear in mind where you are to plant them. There are special dwarf varieties which are ideal for tubs and window boxes and the front of a border. They also form dark green clumps that look pleasant in winter. The taller varieties should be planted in groups if they are not to look silly.

In most places you will be presented with a mixed selection to surprise you with their rich velvety colours in spring. But at a much higher price you can go somewhere where they also stock individual colours. Suttons have a huge selection. I particularly love the primrose-coloured varieties and those deep wine-red ones called Vulcan. Of course the cheap way to get exactly the flower you want is to grow them from seed in May next year, to flower the following May.

Wallflowers are wonderfully unfussy plants. Any soil will suit them and, although I tend to throw in some bonemeal while planting just to give them a head start, they need no tending. They also do not mind semi-shade so those brilliant yellows and whites can greatly improve a north-facing border.

Spring bulbs

Spring bulbs are a real investment. Choose the right sort and they'll need little attention, entrance you from February to May, and return multiplied year after year. Shops and nurseries still have them and there is just time to get them by mail order. Daffodils and narcissi look particularly pretty when naturalized in rough grass or under trees (they appear before the trees have leaves to shade them). I love the tiny ones like N. *lobularis* and N. *canaliculatus*. If you mix the varieties and plant some in shade you will have flowers for longer.

Plant them in scattered clumps – for the natural look throw a bundle on the ground and plant them where they land – at a depth at least twice that of the bulb. All bulbs need food if they are to flourish for years ahead, so dig peat and bonemeal into the soil. Old gardeners always say you should have your daffodil bulbs in by the end of October and tulips by late November.

A bulb catalogue such as Kelway's offers you such a big selection it is tempting to take a few of many varieties. In fact the effect will be more natural if you stick to just a few varieties planted in drifts in long grass or in large groups in the border. *Narcissus* Ice Follies have white outer petals (the perianth) and a short creamy-white cup with frilly edges. It flowers quite early. Binkie comes later and is a lovely soft lemon, becoming almost white. Both grow about sixteen inches tall, so are good for the middle of the border. I find them the most beautiful of all the narcissi. (See April.)

For rockeries or the front of a bed try the breathtaking miniature daffodils like the cyclamineus, aptly named because the petals turn back like a cyclamen, which grow to six inches and are ideal for naturalizing. You could try lovely little white Jenny, golden Tete-à-tete or N. *canaliculatus* which has a white perianth and a deep gold cup. A small bed of these outside your kitchen window, perhaps mixed in with blue anemones and chionodoxa, is bound to raise your spirits in those dark days when winter threatens never to go.

Tulips disappoint me. After one bold appearance they have shot their bolt. You might get them to flower again if you dig them up, but that is a real bore. However, there is a group of little species tulips which will flower on indefinitely. These include *Tulipa fosteriana*, *T. kaufmanniana*, the brilliant sunny yellow and white

T. tarda, and *T. greigii*. They are quite enchanting and being short –
generally six to ten inches – look lovely in rockeries, tubs and
window boxes.

Get digging

My grandmother's saying that you take out of life only what you put
in is particularly apt when it comes to soil. Whatever the soil type in
your garden – you may be lucky enough to have a good medium
loam or unfortunate enough to be landed with back-breaking clay –
the more you work on it to improve both its texture and fertility the
easier it will be to handle and the more verdant your garden will
become. This applies more than ever in vegetable gardening where
you are taking an enormous amount out of the soil. You can remedy
this to a degree by rotating your crops on a three-year scheme. But
the most important task in October is to get digging.

If you still have rows of sprouts, winter lettuces and other vegetables
in the garden, then you must dig the soil as the areas become vacant.
Whatever you do it is important to avoid digging when it is too wet
(the simple test is to see whether the soil clings heavily to your boots)
as this has the effect, particularly with clay, of compacting the soil so
that the drainage gets worse.

Double digging is a term used to describe the traditional English
way of digging over your whole garden so that all the soil is turned
over to a depth of about nine inches. It is then left to weather and to be
broken down by frost over winter. First dig a shallow trench the
width and depth of your spade at one end of the plot leaving the soil
in large lumps (the soil you remove should be carted to the other end).
Then put some compost or manure in the bottom of the trench.
Next, turn over the neighbouring spade's width into the trench.
This will leave another trench behind into which you put manure,
turn over the next spade's width, and so on. When you get to the end
there should be an empty trench into which you put that soil you
have lugged from your first dig. This system is ideal for root vegetables which you will sow next spring. If you fancy something less
complicated just turn the soil over and lay the compost on top.

Few of us have room to make all the compost we need and manure
can be hard to come by; so it might be necessary to do the more
expensive thing and buy garden centre compost. Spent mushroom

compost is excellent as is that based on horse manure. Peat will substantially improve the texture of your soil, particularly if it is heavy clay; but remember that peat contains no nutritional value for the plants so you will have to add compound fertilizer in the spring.

NOVEMBER

FLOWERS, SHRUBS AND TREES

Complete bulb planting.
Start planting trees, roses and shrubs from now until March when the soil is not frosted or waterlogged.
Add compost or bonemeal.
Plant herbaceous plants, protecting with slug pellets. Lift late chrysanthemums indoors to take cuttings in spring. Clear up all borders and lay compost or manure between now and February.
Take hardwood cuttings, in sandy soil outdoors, of shrubs like buddleia, winter jasmine, ribes.
Write for seed catalogues.

VEGETABLES, FRUIT AND HERBS

Plant new fruit bushes and trees; prune after planting. Spray peaches and nectarines before their leaves fall, to control leaf curl. Continue taking cuttings of gooseberries and currants.
Prune older apple and pear trees, also espalier-grown forms. Finish pruning blackberries and raspberries. Be sure that fruit bushes are well protected from birds who get hungry now and can damage buds. Keep digging the soil in your vegetable garden. Add manure and leave the soil rough. Sow first broad beans.

PLANTS UNDER PROTECTION

Give minimal water to all pot plants, but ensure that they are kept moist and in good light.
See that your greenhouse is kept airy so that rot doesn't set in. Remove all dead leaves.
Pot up rooted cuttings made in late summer, also annuals sown in September or October.

OTHER JOBS

Keep cleaning fallen leaves and muck from ponds. Keep net across your pond. Dig a lawn site for sowing in spring. Keep aerating established lawns. Sharpen tools and service the mower.

Tree gazing

URING THIS SEASON, when I only have eyes for trees, I
have but one golden piece of advice: get you to an arboretum
fast before those dazzling colours fade. You may not be
alone. I remember making such an expedition to the famous Westonbirt arboretum near Tetbury in Gloucestershire one Sunday in
November and thinking the idea rather original. When I arrived, I
discovered that over 1,300 car-loads of people had been similarly
inspired. However, in a large place like that the crowds are easily
absorbed. Another November visit was to the Bedgbury Pinetum in
Kent, and yet another to Hillier's arboretum in Hampshire (a rather
'young' arboretum).

In each case, of course, the drive there is half the fun, for the tree
colours by the roadside positively sing out in shades of yellow, red
and rich copper. Take a whole day drinking in the colours as they
change with the light. In late afternoon there is mist about, mingling
with smoke from autumn bonfires. When the cool sunlight breaks
through catching the last yellow and crimson tips of the maples
you will not regret you came.

Moving from a young arboretum – in which many of the trees are
only ten or so years old and can give you quite an idea of what the
trees you plant in your own garden could grow up to look like –
to an old one like Westonbirt is like becoming Sleeping Beauty.
Close your eyes and lo: the forest has grown up and reached a height
and density you could hardly imagine. Westonbirt was begun in
1829 and contains an estimated 2,000 varieties of 550 species.

The main area was first planted in 1855 and its development from
that time well into this century coincided with a period of feverish
plant hunting, when every week, it seemed, some explorer would
return with yet another azalea, maple (acer) or magnolia from some
remote place like the Himalayas or China. David Douglas returned
from America bringing a Douglas fir which is now 103 feet tall.

In November it is the maples that steal the scene with their vivid
scarlets or golds, so bright that from a distance the small ones look
like groups of flowering azaleas. Maples are particularly interesting
to town gardeners for many of them are quite small and, assuming
you only have room for one tree, they satisfy most needs. They look
wonderful from spring to November and maintain fine shapes even
when the leaves have fallen.

It is difficult to know where to begin with maples. Hilliers list over 150 in their catalogue, including vast numbers of *Acer palmatum*, or Japanese maple, which grow into manageable-sized garden trees. I was specially struck by *A. palmatum* Osakazuki, with its vivid red and green autumn colour. But if you want a fresh golden colour in summer followed by deeper gold in autumn choose *A. palmatum* Aureum.

Acer japonicum Vitifolium is one of the most brilliant and *A. japonicum* Aconitifolium had enchantingly delicate, sharply cut leaves which turn deep crimson tinted with gold in autumn. *Acer negundo* Variegatum has white variegated foliage. It grows fast to about eighteen feet which is a perfect size for a smallish garden. I have it growing in front of my house. *A. palmatum* Albomarginatum has green leaves with white variegation in a striking red, tipped with cream. The actual silver maple (*A. saccharinum*) looks as if flecked with silver dust when the wind blows. But it does grow large and should only be planted where space can be spared.

Another brilliant small tree with very fine shape is rhus. Its feathery leaves which ripple in the breeze are lovely all summer, but when October arrives it puts on its glad rags with a show of vivid crimson lasting well into this month – a display that will take your breath away. *Rhus typhina* is the most popular variety and as it is unfussy about soil and atmospheric pollution it is a well-established favourite of mine.

Tree planting

When I bought my first house, one of the attractions was a huge sycamore tree which grew in the yard of a butcher's shop backing on to my garden. Granted, I cursed it when every year I weeded out hundreds of sycamore saplings and raked the dead leaves, but it was home to many sparrows and as it blocked the view of the back of the shops, made me feel as if I was in the country. Then one day in summer I returned home and immediately felt something was wrong. I went out into the garden and horror! the tree was gone. The cheery men clearing the site where it had been were unimpressed by my almost speechless shock. They thought I would be pleased and, besides, the butcher's shop needed to expand. It seemed callous to blame the butcher but my street had lost something irreplaceable and wonderful. The loss to us humans was as nothing compared to that of the poor sparrows, for in town alternative accommodation doesn't come easy for them.

Thoughtless murders like this happen every day. The Tree Council estimates that about fifty million trees have been lost in the past twenty-five years and the same amount will go before the century is out, dying from disease, old age and because of town development. They are not being replaced nearly fast enough. So think how you might improve the landscape by planting a tree.

Of course there is a limit to what you can do in your own garden if you live in a town, but you could join some local amenity society and badger your local authority to raise money to plant trees in different areas. There are so many bits of waste ground where a plane or a beech would wonderfully improve the view for generations to come.

If you have a long garden, then you really have the scope for proper big trees like limes, poplars (don't plant a poplar near a wall as the roots are intrusive), beech, birch or perhaps an exotic catalpa to enhance the view for yourself and others. Send for a catalogue listing likely trees (see Appendix VI).

Evergreen trees

In November we admire the many trees which are looking spectacularly lovely with their autumn tints. But by Christmas time you will be appreciating the evergreens. They may look a bit drab now, but they won't play second fiddle for long. It's important to plant trees which somehow act as foils to each other, making a combination of different shapes and colours which will be of interest all year round.

In town we tend to lack space. So trees that grow up rather than out are a boon. There are many varieties of cypress which can look wonderful. The most popular nowadays is the Leyland cypress (*Cupresocyparis leylandii*) which grows at a spanking pace and is used a lot to make thick hedges. I have to admit that I find the yellowish variety a bit garish. But if you want a quick growth, then the ordinary, silvery green one is for you.

One particularly pretty Lawson cypress is called Intertexta. It grows straight up but has branches that drip in a distinctive way reminding me of paintings by Altdorfer. If you want to be reminded of Leonardo, however, you must make for an Italian cypress (*Cupressus semper-virens*). These wonderful, tall, dark trees which dot the Italian landscape complementing the soft, rounded, silvery olive trees, are among my favourites. They look most impressive if planted in a group.

An evergreen which can look fine when mixed with deciduous trees is the Irish yew (*Taxus baccata* Fastigiata). This is a wider growing dark tree which is much associated with churchyards. However, when combined with more colourful company it can look extremely striking and attractive. When your tree arrives by post from the nursery, look after it so that it gets a good start. If it arrives during the frost or when the ground is water-logged don't attempt to plant it. Cover its roots with some sacking or newspaper and keep it in a shed until a warmer drier day for planting arrives.

Choosing a tree

There is something deeply exciting about planting a tree. But choosing a specimen tree for your garden can be agonizing. It is hard to imagine what it will look like in five, ten or twenty years' time. Will it dominate the garden leaving you to find plants which don't mind shade or will it just provide that point of focus and uplift which your garden needs? But choose you must, and now is as good a time as any. The deciduous leaves have not all dropped, yet there's oodles of time to plant. You can do so until March as long as the soil is not rigid with frost or waterlogged.

The only cause for haste is that if you order a particular tree in January you stand the chance of being disappointed as your local garden centre or nursery may have been cleaned out. This happened to me one year, thus wasting another twelve precious growing months before I could dig in a magical, much-longed-for *Cornus kousa chinensis*.

Cornus kousa is one of the dogwood family and so its great feature is not so much the flowers (which are insignificant) as the white flower-like bracts which cover it like a wedding bonnet in June. There is a brilliant specimen at Nymans near Handcross in West Sussex.

I am intrigued by the maidenhair tree (*Ginkgo biloba*). This columnar tree with round notched leaves like maidenhair fern is not widely grown. It has the distinction of coming from a family which has resolutely declined to evolve (there have been ginkgos just like the one you might select growing for more than a hundred million years).

Another soft yellow tree is *Gleditschia triacanthos*, or honey locust. It grows quite tall but spreads charmingly with its feathery soft green leaves. In my favourite variety called Sunburst the young leaves are bright yellow, becoming a limey yellow in summer.

Robinia pseudoacacia has similarly floaty, frondlike leaves which shimmer in a breeze. The variety called Frisia is a striking yellow turning to gold in autumn. Driving down Constitution Hill I notice that the Queen has a terrific specimen beyond the Palace garden wall.

Silver trees

Silver plants of all kinds fascinate and entrance me and silver trees especially. If you have space at the bottom of the garden try a group of *Eucalyptus gunnii* or cedar gums which will grow very fast and look wonderfully striking with their grey-blue foliage. When mature they have rather slim, feathery leaves but when young they bear strangely primitive-looking rounded leaves which are a flower arranger's delight.

One of the best known silver trees must be the weeping silver pear (*Pyrus salicifolia* Pendula) which Vita Sackville-West made the centre-piece of her white garden at Sissinghurst. It is a truly enchanting tree with branches of silver, willowy leaves which look feather-light and hang down elegantly. It can look lovely alone on a lawn and grows about fifteen feet tall. On advice from a garden designer I planted three together in a clump with their trunks literally a foot apart in a friend's rather large garden. The result so far is rather spectacular for they are growing up together in a great silver clump. There is a non-weeping variety which is also beautiful and grows to nearer twenty feet. Both trees have little white flowers in April, as does the snow pear (*Pyrus nivalis*) which is an equally lovely tree with branches stretching out horizontally. Although called pears none of these bear edible fruit.

I adore silver birches of all kinds. There is something so delicate about their rustling leaves, and the elegance of the silver bark is very striking when the leaves have gone. They do not cast heavy shade so they make good garden trees if you have the space. Our native silver birch (*Betula pendula*) will grow to over twenty feet. For a specimen tree placed, perhaps, in the middle of a lawn, you might try the *B.p.* Youngii variety which forms a dome-shaped weeping tree and is truly lovely. It only grows to around fifteen feet, so it is perfect for small gardens.

When planting your trees choose a day when the soil is not water-logged and dig a deepish, wide hole. In it place the tree roots and a strong stake to which you will attach the tree. Firm the stake down in the ground and then fill up the hole with earth and good compost, adding some bonemeal to set it off well. Firm the ground down around the tree by stamping with your boots as you would with any shrub, making sure that the stake is firm enough to keep your tree upright in the winter gales. After that water the tree and make sure that, if Mother Nature fails to do so, you keep it watered regularly.

Winter window boxes

It always amazes me how sporting geraniums can be. Quite often mine have bravely flowered on into November – a shadow of their summer selves but still a stirring sight. The same could not be said of many other bedding plants and generally, by now, most window boxes, planted out with such enthusiasm in June, look a very sorry sight.

So what should one do with them? Nobody wants a bedraggled window box with nothing to show for itself throughout the winter months when you need its cheer more than ever. Spring bulbs will not make an appearance until March or April, so in the meantime some good vivid foliage is the answer.

Of course there are varieties of flowers which have fine foliage for winter. I am thinking particularly of wallflowers which will look very gay in a box in spring if you choose the short varieties. Their deep green leaves liven up any garden in January and February before even the suggestion of a flower has appeared. But a more long-term scheme is to plant little evergreen shrubs and ivies. These can live on year in, year out, in a tub or a window box, but every

June you will have to scoop carefully around their roots to renew the earth in order to plant your annuals. They will also need regular fertilizer in their growing period as they will get precious little from the earth in the box. I always incorporate a lot of my old standby, bonemeal, when renewing the soil in June.

Plainly it is sensible to think of shrubs which will survive a dry spell, as window boxes dehydrate so easily. Most silver-leafed shrubs are ideal. I have found *Senecio greyi* a real stalwart here and it should last you a good five years.

A rosemary bush will stay evergreen, provide a good background for your summer flowers and have the added advantage of giving you sprigs to liven up the roast lamb. Bush herbs smell lovely, so you might consider some low-growing lavender like the silver *Lavandula lanata* which forms an attractive bush, or the compact *L.* Hidcote. Different varieties of silver santolina, or cotton lavender, can look marvellous forming soft rounded clumps. *S. incana* Nana is good and showy.

The perfect silver window box shrub, to my mind, is little *Hebe* Pagei. It grows about a foot tall and has many tiny little silver leaves on stems which will tumble over the box side. Like all hebes it can retain water and so will do well.

Protect the tender

Climatically speaking, most town dwellers live in cloud-cuckoo land. So protected are we by the shelter from neighbouring buildings and the warmer climate than one gets in the countryside, that it is easy to become lazy if, for instance, your geraniums have survived a mild winter out of doors. Then suddenly you are caught out. A really cold spell will kill off all those tender plants at a stroke.

One such cold spell occurred over a Christmas holiday when I was away. Fortunately, rather as an afterthought, I had dragged my beloved oleander bushes – which had survived previous winters in a plastic greenhouse – into the kitchen to sit out my absence. They survived unscathed but the geraniums, which had managed many years in a cold greenhouse against the house, were blackened corpses on my return.

So, make sure you are not caught out in the same way. One

solution of course is a very light heat in the greenhouse, but that gets expensive over a long period. Geraniums (or pelargoniums) can put up with quite low temperatures as long as they are not allowed to freeze for long. So, at the risk of your home becoming a jungle, pack as many as you can into a few good-sized pots and bring them in to sit on your lightest window ledge. Don't put them near a radiator or they will keep growing in a leggy way. And give them very little water. The same treatment applies to fuchsias and other precious plants which would survive a mild winter.

Don't be surprised if the geranium leaves drop a bit – that is normal in winter. You should not give them any food during the really dark months. Then in late February feed them some kind of liquid fertilizer with high potash content to get the flowers going. That way they should be blooming happily by the time you put them out again in May or June.

Other candidates for protection are dahlias and begonias, which you should certainly have brought in by now. Dahlia tubers should be kept in a box in a cool place, perhaps with some peat to cover. Begonias should be left in some peaty mixture in the cool (an ideal temperature is around 45°F) to be potted up again in the spring. Give them a little moisture to stop them drying up.

The romance of lilac

When planning your tree planting, spare a thought for the lilac tree – if you don't, then when May arrives you will wish you had. Towards the end of May any garden which does not have its single lilac tree in full bloom of brilliant white (my favourite), mauve or purple flowers feels positively undressed. We had white lilacs in the garden when I was a child and to me they evoke everything that is fresh and lovely about an English country garden. On top of that their smell is such heaven that a small spray put into a bowl of water by your bed can transform the atmosphere.

There are many shrubby varieties of species lilacs from the east, but the common lilac which is so frequently seen in English gardens is *Syringa vulgaris*, the European lilac which has been with us since the sixteenth century. It grows to be a small tree which, rather depending on the variety (and a good catalogue will tell you) can grow up to about ten feet tall. In itself it is not a particularly beautiful tree once the flowers have gone, so I feel its place should be down at the bottom of the garden.

Nowadays there are so many varieties of S. *vulgaris* – they range in both single and double flowers from blueish shades through the traditional lilac colours to pink, red and purple. My most recent discovery from Notcutts is Primrose which is exactly the colour it suggests. Those charming soft yellow heads come as such a surprise, and I must admit to finding them very attractive indeed. Monique Lemoine is a lovely double white raised by Lemoine who seem responsible for so many of the interesting colours. Another Lemoine variety is Firmament which is an extraordinarily lovely sky blue and comes out quite early in May; Lemoine also produced Michael Buchner which is the nearest any double variety gets to a true blue.

Lilacs have the advantage of being pretty unfussy about where they are grown. Obviously they will start off better if planted with a good compost. But once they are there, just put some manure around their feet every winter and they will thrive. Cut back any suckers that appear from the base and if you want to prune the tree back into a good shape do so after it has flowered, removing the straggly shoots. The best way of all to prune is of course to cut flowering branches and decorate your home.

Talking garbage

Every American kitchen worth its salt has two waste bins, unceremoniously labelled 'garbage' and 'trash'. This division is more aesthetic than ecological; the garbage, being smelly, decomposing matter is emptied twice a week, the trash only once. We British, with our generally cooler summers, have not felt such a need. However, if you are a gardener and do not have a special kitchen bin labelled 'compost' into which you religiously drop potato peelings, tea leaves and all vegetable matter, you should be deeply ashamed.

It is a truism that one can never have enough compost, and particularly so in town. What's more, faced with a small plot, there is a strong temptation to give space priority to the children's sand pit or rockery, when in fact space put over to compost will repay every inch. This is the season of the big dig. Soil not under cultivation should be dug and turned over, be strewn with compost or manure and then left to weather over the winter months. Come spring the frost and earthworms will have done their stuff and your soil should be crumbly and manageable.

To keep your heap both neat and well aerated, it's sensible to build a good compost box. This should be about three feet square and three feet high with walls made of any available material – brick, wood-slats, wire mesh on corner stakes – so long as it is constructed to let in the air at the sides and, particularly, underneath. For those with less space or who lack materials there are the ready-made compost bins, while for those with space to spare, the ideal is a twin box: then, while you are using one compost crop, you can be making some more. Your compost must also be kept moist but not saturated, so a cover made of old carpet or sacking is a help.

Almost anything that has grown can break down in a well-balanced compost heap. From the garden, throw in lawn mowings (though not if they have been subjected to weedkillers), vegetable plants, weeds and tree-leaves, though avoid evergreens and twiggy matter. From the kitchen, use anything from apple cores to old newspaper. The important thing is to mix the ingredients well. Too many leaves will take a long while to decompose alone, but should do so easily when mixed with green matter.

Mix your ingredients before putting them on the heap and lay the mixture in layers about six to nine inches deep. Between these layers add a thin coating of some activator like horse manure or one of the proprietary compost makers like Garotta which – particularly in winter when nitrogen is scarce – speed up the process no end.

In high summer a well-made compost heap should take about twelve weeks to produce good compost – that's according to the Soil Association. Mine has always taken longer. In winter things slow down and if you start a compost heap now it should be conveniently ready by March or April.

DECEMBER

FLOWERS, TREES AND SHRUBS

Keep planting roses, trees and shrubs.
On frosty nights protect tender plants like hebes
with sacking or newspaper. Move young trees, shrubs
and herbaceous plants. Dig far from the stem or trunk
and wrap the root ball in paper so the earth does not
fall off in the move. Divide overcrowded plants like
day lilies. Tidy up all beds. Start ordering flower
seeds. Firm down plants whose roots are loosened by
frost. Pinch tips of sweet pea seedlings sown in
autumn above the second pair of leaves to make
them branch. Be sure ties and stakes are firm on
climbers and shrubs.

VEGETABLES, FRUIT AND HERBS

Begin spraying fruit trees and bushes with tar
oil and wash. Plant fruit trees and bushes in good
weather. In fine dry weather keep digging manure and
compost into the ground where you are to sow in spring.
Mulch herb bushes if weather turns severe.
Start ordering vegetable seeds. Sow more broad beans.

PLANTS UNDER PROTECTION

Keep watering of house-plants down to a minimum.
Keep them near the light. Keep Christmas plants as
cool as possible. Ventilate the greenhouse in good
weather and avoid fungus by always removing dead leaves.
Bring bowls of bulbs indoors from the plunge bed
when the shoots are 2 in. tall. Line your greenhouse
with polythene if you want to insulate it more.
If you have heat you can sow annuals like
antirrhinums to flower in May. Put rubber balls on
your pool to stop the ice cracking the sides. Feed
fish a little. Rake leaves off lawns and avoid walking
on them in frost. Take the opportunity to clean and
sharpen your tools and have the mower serviced.

Picking seeds

A S A CHILD I remember seeing my mother curled up in an armchair, her nose deep into the Suttons catalogue, choosing her seeds. She could never be disturbed while at this vital task. She always bought her seeds by post and, since gardening is steeped in tradition, I did just the same, when I finally had my own garden. Since then I have been more promiscuous, trying seeds from Unwins, Dobies etc., as well as Suttons. But whatever the brand, I have never considered buying seeds over the counter.

So it came as a shock to learn that of the ten million odd gardeners in Britain who buy seeds, only one and a half million – representing the bigger spending end of the market – buy them by mail: the rest pick up the more limited offerings of their local shop. These inno-cents just don't know what they are missing, and if you're one of them, you should remedy this and write off for a catalogue – or two – at once (see Appendix VI).

Seed catalogues are the last of the big bargains. At no cost at all you get a book, one hundred and twenty or so pages long, giving details of all the different varieties, their various merits or limitations, when to sow, how to store, how to plan your plot, what you should be up to month by month and so on. All are beautifully illustrated. Some even run to recipes using home-grown vegetables. Suttons and Dobies have the largest selections of all, but other firms may have a particular speciality. I always rush to the Unwins catalogue for their sweet peas. They are such favourites of mine and the family firm of Unwins have specialized in them for the past seventy-six years, often naming their creations after members of the family (Sally Unwin is a specially pretty and vigorous bright pink variety). They have a pure white bloom called Diamond Wedding which is very sweetly scented, a brilliant mix of salmon and pink called Sheila Macqueen, the most captivating soft pink flower called Fiona, and a new salmon-coloured, scented variety called Frances Perry, bred and named by Charles Unwin.

When looking through the flower section of your catalogue it is tempting to order everything. But certain flowers will be especially worthwhile, even with quite limited space. For instance your corner shop probably won't have a wide selection of sweet pea seeds when the time comes and this year it might be fun to grow white ones only, or a mix of, say, soft pink and white or deep purple and white.

Similarly, if you are willing to grow under glass with a little heat – and here a window sill will do – think of all those bedding plants like petunias. You will be easily able to buy expensive mixtures come June. But a glance at a good catalogue will show you what infinitely more interesting varieties you could grow from seed choosing your own colour scheme (when Chelsea won the cup I had a friend who decked out his window boxes entirely in blue and white petunias).

Another flower which I love to grow is lavatera, or mallow. The Silver Cup variety is soft pink and there are interesting white varieties. They bloom for a long time throughout the summer. Nicotiana is another obvious choice and again there are so many to choose from which you would not be able to buy as plants. Over the years I have grown many zonal geraniums from seed. The plants are very expensive to buy in the shops, so I increase my stock from cuttings, and get a larger selection this way.

Then think of the perennials (see June) which you can sow in June to flower the following summer. Wallflowers, for a start, are easy to grow from seed and by the time you sow them the shelves of your greenhouse will be empty as you will have bedded out all the annuals. Lupins, delphiniums, hollyhocks, day lilies (hemerocallis), Canterbury bells and glorious spikes of primrose-yellow verbascum: these stalwarts of the herbaceous border which are so expensive in the shops can all be grown easily from summer-sown seed and, again, you will have a much larger collection. Think also about growing violas and pansies which, to my mind, make infinitely prettier edging plants than annuals like lobelia, and go on from year to year.

If you fancy a wild-looking garden with flowers seeding themselves thither and yon, buy some foxglove (digitalis) seeds and some columbine (aquilegia) which will seed themselves everywhere once you have got a few plants growing. Try also valerian which will tuck into the tiny crevices of a wall and grow lovely bright pink flowers that will bloom long into summer.

When it comes to vegetables the same rules apply. Make for the ones that you are not likely to find on sale round the corner at the same time that yours come to ripen. There are so many interesting types of cucumber (even charming little round ones which I have grown and which taste rather sweet), bizarre varieties of lettuce, stringless beans, climbing – rather than low-growing – French beans, golden courgettes, delicious tiny marrows called Little Gem, and so on. The fun of growing your own is not just that they taste better but also that they are genuinely different.

The glory of lilies

Were I allowed only one flower on my desert island, I would choose a Regale lily. I have clumps of them in my garden jammed in tubs with the spring bulbs. Every year they rear up to amaze me yet again when their long pink buds open to exquisite trumpet flowers (creamy, shading to a yellow throat) and enchant me with their heady smell.

Lilies are a godsend to balcony gardeners. Though they look majestic in herbaceous borders they appear to grow just as well in tubs – better sometimes. In a tub you can, with the help of peat, compost and sand, create the excellent drainage which lilies absolutely demand. Site the tub near the house – in at least half sunlight – and you will get the full benefit of their soothing smell on summer evenings. Except for Madonna lilies, which are contrary in many ways, lilies should be planted any time from now till March, though not when the ground is frosty or waterlogged.

Try to plan so that your selection spans the summer. You might kick off with *L. monadelphum* (vivid primrose yellow), Regale and Enchantment (a rich purply red) – all flowering in June. In July Royal Gold (a yellow version of Regale) and *L. martagon* (white or purple) would take over, making way for orange tiger lilies and pink and white *L. speciosum melpomene* in August and September. Plant your lilies about six inches deep. They like cool damp feet and good food. So enrich the soil with a handful of bonemeal and give them a good mulch of manure or compost, repeating this in the spring.

Lilies come in varying, very different, shapes. There are the trumpet shapes like *L. regale* whose petals curl out gently at the end. There are the Turk's caps, the petals of which curl back completely, such as the vivid orange *L. henryi*, the more speckled *L. pardalinum* and of course the wonderful bright speckled deep pink and white *L. martagon* which bears a good twenty flowers on a stem. There are those which open their petals wide like a star such as *L. auratum*, those which droop elegantly like *L. canadense*, and those which look up to the sky. They differ greatly in the number of flowers they bear and whether they carry them up the length of the stem or all in a crowd at the top. The species from the Himalayas, Japan, China, America, Korea, Greece and many other places, have been bred and cross-bred to produce an enormous number of variations for you to wonder over and choose from.

If you buy your lilies by post you will have access to a large selection. When choosing from a catalogue always make a note of how high they will grow. Most of my favourites like the lovely yellow Destiny will grow to around three feet tall but there are many such as the amazing Imperial Silver with its tiny rust-coloured spots and its relation, Imperial Gold, which is the same but with streaks of yellow, which will romp up to five feet tall. If you have a place in the garden where a dramatic six foot flower would look good, then don't fail to buy the graceful and majestic *L. auratum*. This is a white open flower with golden star markings which also possesses amazing rusty speckles.

In winter, when your lilies have died back, you can lift them or take them from their tubs and propagate from a few of the bulbs by gently removing the fleshy outside scales and planting them in pots in a mixture of peat and sand, leaving just the very top showing. Put them in a warmish place, keep them moist and in two months they should have formed baby plants. Plant these out in good compost. You can also grow species lilies such as *L. regale* from seed, but as they take two to three years to flower you must be more patient than I can manage to be.

Holly and ivy

Just about now I deeply regret my lack of a holly bush. I have little to be proud of when it comes to ivy either. As both of these are particularly attractive all year round in town gardens – minding neither sun nor shade – and are a must come Christmas, it's worth planning to plant some in the next few months. You won't have enough holly and ivy for next year's decorations, but in a few years' time you will bless the day you planted.

Holly, or ilex, is not just the traditional dark green English holly (*I. aquifolium*) with spikey leaves and red berries. It comes in many varieties, some of them beautifully variegated and some not spikey at all. Most, however, are evergreen and make fine, if slow-growing, small trees. The berries are born on the female bush. So to achieve them you must have a male as well – or fix it that your neighbour does.

Though I love the old English holly, you might prefer to plan a variegated one which will look attractive all year. Here the choice is wide. *I. aquifolium* Argenteomarginata is the silver-margined holly. It bears lovely berries and also comes in a very attractive weeping form called Perry's Weeping. There are many hollies with gold margins, one of the best being *I. aquifolium* Madame Briot which has specially good berries as well. Another fine one is *I. altaclarensis* Golden King which again bears fine berries and has few spines. *I. altaclarensis* Lawsoniana is particularly lovely as the gold and green blend into each other giving the appearance of having been painted. If you really go for gold try *I. aquifolium* Golden Milkboy which has leaves more gold than green.

With ivy or hedera, you have a similarly wide choice. All are ever-green, some have berries, some have variegated leaves and some plain, while the size and shape of the leaves varies a good deal. *Hedera helix* is the common ivy which comes in many forms. I am specially fond of *H. h.* Goldheart. It has small heart-shaped leaves with bright yellow centres. It will grow well up walls, but also thrives in window boxes and tubs. An urn with nothing but Goldheart spilling down its sides is particularly cheering at this time of year. It is also a joy for flower arranging.

A good fast-growing variegated ivy is *H. canariensis* Gloire de Marengo. It has wide leaves with silvery margins shading in to a deep green centre. It is often recommended for growing up a trellis. With even larger leaves *H. colchica* Dentata Variegata has marvel-lously bold gold and green markings. I use little Silver Queen a lot in flower arrangements. Its leaves are the traditional three-lobed ivy shape and are delightfully smudged with irregular dashes of silver. I grow it up a wall, but it also makes good ground cover and a very attractive indoor plant.

Christmas decor

In the middle of this month, all thoughts are on Christmas decoration and however much you can cull from the garden you are probably going to have to buy a Christmas tree. Take time choosing this as some can already be dropping their spines by the time they reach your corner shop. If it is recently cut the spines will be springy and there is a chance it will do you well until twelfth night. Put it in water the minute you buy it for the more water your tree has, the less it will drop needles.

When you do bring it indoors to decorate, place it in a bucket of moist sand or earth and make sure it stays moist. Place it as far from a radiator as possible. You can, of course, buy a rooted tree in a little tub, but most of them seem to be very small. However, they grow quickly and, provided they are not kept too long indoors each Christmas, can soldier on year after year.

I have a very attractive bay-tree which spends all year in a large terra cotta tub on my back patio. At Christmastime, it is trundled indoors for a short spell in a coolish spot, and then decorated. The glossy evergreen leaves look so attractive – it has rather a Christmas tree shape anyway – and so far it is none the worse for wear. Bay, however, is not so good if you intend to use it as a cut leaf, because it dies off easily. So if you are making a garland – which can look so enchanting hung on a wall – stick to the conifers or holly or yew, which do last much longer.

If your garden does not come up trumps it's worth taking note and ordering some shrubs to plant in the next month or so which will stand you in good stead for Christmas to come. Variegated evergreens such as the hollies and ivies I have described are especially lovely now. But the variegated shrub which outstrips them all is elaeagnus.

There are some enchanting varieties of holly such as *Ilex aquifolium* Silver Queen, which has silver markings and also bears berries. This is a long-term investment as holly grows slowly. Variegated ivies like the little Goldheart grow fast and are a boon for decorating all year. I am particularly keen on one called *Hedera colchica* Dentata Variegata whose smudgy lemon and green markings look as if they've been painted by hand.

The yellow-leaved *E. pungens* Maculata with its quite thin lines of green will transform any arrangement. It must be used sparingly as the bushes grow slowly. Once established, your bush will entrance you all year, but never more than on freezing February mornings when the rest of the garden looks dead and its golden leaves somehow light up in the faint rays of early sunshine.

Elaeagnus also comes in a non-variegated form which has deep grey-green leaves with marvellous silver colour on the reverse. This, too, is ideal for flower arrangements as it provides attractive background and lasts wonderfully long in water.

A shrub which bursts into its own just now is *Garrya elliptica*. In summer this evergreen with its matt grey-green leaves is pleasant enough and has the particular advantage that it is happy growing against a north wall. But in November it produces very delicate catkins in a soft green which then turn yellower as the pollen appears, hanging six to nine inches long. It is very effective in arrangements and you can cut bits from November to March.

If you lack evergreen silver-leafed foliage, this should be remedied fast. I so enjoy the gloriously frothy effect of my little lavender bushes. *Lavandula spica* (Dutch lavender) is a particularly good silver variety which will grow more than two feet. Snippings of it stuck into oasis (which you can buy from any flower shop and is a must for decorating) along with blue rue and silver cotton lavender (santolina) can look enchanting as part of a table decoration.

Finally, Christmas decor is not complete without berries. Many of them are over now – with the obvious exception of holly – though some of my pyracantha is still quite usable. But the little bush I find a boon just now is evergreen *Skimmia japonica*. Skimmia has a snag in that you must buy a male and female shrub in order to get berries. But they look delightful sitting side by side and besides, the rich red berries now will give you sweetly scented white flowers next April.

Save Christmas plants

Nearly every Christmas my Grannie and I seem to contrive between us to murder a cyclamen. So convinced are we of the other's scattiness that the hapless plant receives a constant double dosage of water and rots away without a murmur. Cyclamen, though ravishing, are difficult at the best of times. I'm sure that all over the country similar silent deaths occur at the hands of over-eager novices who have been suddenly landed with a plant they haven't a clue how to care for.

The shops are now full of cyclamen, poinsettias and azaleas, which all make lovely presents and decorations. Remember that by the time a plant comes into your hands it will have already undergone a series of shocks. Having been raised in a snug commercial greenhouse under ideal conditions of heat, light and humidity, it has been rudely transported, over lengthy distances perhaps, to a wholesaler and then to your local shopkeeper who proceeds proudly and gormlessly to display it outside, come hail or shine. It may look healthy, but illness could be imminent.

Extreme sources of heat and cold are death to house-plants. So, although these three all like good light and should be kept near the window in day-time, take them off the window sill at night so that they don't catch the frost. Ideally, these plants want a room temperature around 50°–55°F. They should be kept well out of draughts. Similarly, it is crucial to avoid putting your plant on, or too close to, a hot radiator.

If you want to keep your plants for next year follow these instructions. With cyclamen – which some people call the buy-and-die-plant – wait until the flowers are over, then let it dry out and store it in a cool place away from frost. Come July when new growth appears you should re-pot it in John Innes No 2 compost, water it and place it in the warmth and light; then you should, with luck, have flowers for next Christmas.

Poinsettias (*Euphorbia pulcherrima*) are easier in my opinion. They are generally potted in peaty soil, so the danger here is that they might dry out. Their actual flowers are tiny and insignificant: it's the colourful bracts – nowadays available in white and pink as well as scarlet – which draw the crowds. Having given of their best, the bracts and leaves will drop. At this point cut the branches back to around four inches and keep the plant in a dry, warm place. When new growth begins, re-pot the plant using fresh John Innes No 2 in perhaps a size larger pot. Once the plant is growing strongly – say, after two months – it should have a liquid feed. Keep it in a place where it gets good, even, natural light – but no artificial light. It has a delicate timing mechanism which only tells it to flower after a month which has a certain number of hours of darkness.

Few people have not had problems with azaleas. The little *Azalea indica* may well flower beautifully but then the buds will drop off. This may be no fault of yours; the plant may have had a rough ride; but for best results remember to keep it well watered. Some people give their azaleas a regular plunge in a bowl of water to ensure that all the peat – which easily dries out – gets well watered. You can put your azalea out of doors in summer, plunged in a peaty bed. When autumn comes you should bring it under cover before the frosts arrive, re-potted in peat or a peat-based compost.

Finally – watering. People unused to house-plants tend to be nervous and water little and often – which may water-log the plant, whose roots thus deprived of oxygen will die – or they only dampen the surface, leaving the roots to dry out. A rare soaking is better.

Grow heathers

The thing I love most about gardening is the eternal sense of discovery: the way you come across a perfectly common shrub or flower as if for the first time and become completely obsessed. It was that way with me and heathers. They had never interested me much, but when my sister moved into a country cottage in Yorkshire and asked for my thoughts on the garden I suggested she grow heathers; she is no gardener and they were said to be trouble-free. Slyly, she flattered me into taking on the job; and thus I embarked on a journey round heather gardens (you should make an effort to see the lovely one at Kew) and it was a rare voyage of discovery.

There are a wealth of different heathers. They are evergreen, and if your selection is chosen carefully will provide a display of flowers throughout the year. They also look particularly pretty when combined with little shrubs such as small hebes – *H. pinguifolia* Pagei or *H. rakaiensis* are good – and with dwarf conifers such as junipers and *chamaecyparis*, or false cypress, to make a miniature garden. Once planted, heathers grow out sideways forming a ground cover that deters even the boldest weed. Their flowers are delicate and enchanting but in many cases their leaves – which vary from deep silver-green to a bright yellow – are equally spectacular. It is important to get the juxtaposition of leaves just right. Similarly, conifers vary from silver-blue (such as the junipers Blue Star and

Blue Carpet) to golden yellow (such as *Chamaecyparis* Minima Aurea).

Heathers fall into three main groups. There is the *Calluna vulgaris* group which are variations on the common moorland heather, the *Daboecia* group and the *Ericas*. Now I have to admit one snag. With the exception of the *Erica carnea* group, all heathers – like azaleas and rhododendrons – hate a limey soil. So it is important to put a good quantity of peat into your soil. Don't buy too many plants as they are easy to grow from rooted cuttings which you should take next July. This is both satisfying and economical, as heathers are not cheap. I love *Erica carnea* Aurea with its golden spring foliage which becomes flecked with red in winter. Ruby Glow has a bronzy leaf setting off its pink flowers. The largest group of summer flowerers is *Calluna vulgaris*, or ling. Double white *Alba plena* is sure to bring you luck, while H. E. Beale delights me with its light pink sprays. Gold Haze has white flowers in late summer, but its golden foliage stays all year round. Similarly, Robert Chapman, whose purple flowers come in late summer, has foliage which changes from gold to orange to red as the year progresses.

Grow pips

Rainy days in the Christmas holidays can sap one's inventive powers. Once the new games have been well and truly tried, the children become restless. So think of an entertaining scheme: they could grow plants from pips. Plants like avocadoes used only to be available in large towns like London. Now they are pretty well all-pervasive. And what to do with these mammoth stones? Grow an avocado plant of course.

The keys to successful plant rearing from seed are temperature, humidity and light. So you do need a propagator of some sort. This is a glass dome which makes a mini-greenhouse, protecting plants from excessive draughts and temperature change and keeping them moist. It can be as sophisticated as the smart thermostatically-controlled affairs or as rudimentary as a polythene bag or a jam jar placed over a plant. So for your holiday challenge, why not start off either a pineapple or an avocado? Here are the instructions.

Pineapple: Cut the topnot off with a disk of flesh one inch thick, leave it for forty-eight hours, with the flesh uppermost, to dry out. Fill a wide but shallow pot with well-drained compost (soil-less cutting compost with sand added is ideal) leaving a layer of crocks at the bottom.

The pot should be at least two inches wider than the pineapple top. Just before planting, sprinkle the cut surface with water and perhaps a little rooting powder. Plant the top with the slice of flesh just covered. Water with tepid water (never use cold). Place in a warm spot (70°–80° F) in a propagator or over a radiator with a polythene bag over its head. The first sign that it is rooting will be when new leaves appear in the centre of the crown. When it's obviously well established move it to its permanent home which should be as warm and sunny as possible.

Avocado: Soak the stone for forty-eight hours in tepid water. Fill a jam jar with tepid water and suspend your stone over the top by sticking matchsticks or hairpins into either side to prop it up. The wide base should be just in the water. Then place in a warm spot like an airing cupboard, checking the water level frequently. The root appears first; and only when the shoot begins need you bring it into light. It may take anything from ten to thirty days to germinate. If nothing happens then you probably have a dud, so it's worth starting two at once. You need not transfer the plant to a pot of compost until the roots are very well developed. Unless stopped the plant will grow straight upwards. So to get a bushy effect nip out the top of the shoot once it has developed a side shoot.

Citrus Fruits (oranges, lemons, limes): Take pips from a ripe fruit and plant them in any seed compost in a temperature of 60°–70° F in a propagator of some sort – say a jam jar with drainage crocks in the bottom and with cellophane on top. Sow the pips so that they are covered with the compost and put somewhere warm, perhaps on the radiator. When little leaves show, carefully take the pip out and replant in a pot. Sow several pips at once as they probably won't all germinate, and don't expect them to bear fruit like the parent plant. As you are probably growing your tree for decoration, this is not much of a problem.

JANUARY

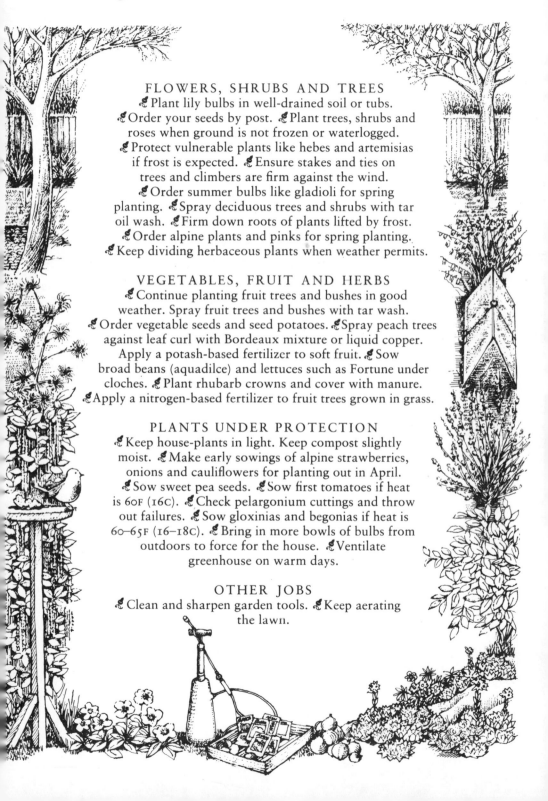

FLOWERS, SHRUBS AND TREES

Plant lily bulbs in well-drained soil or tubs. Order your seeds by post. Plant trees, shrubs and roses when ground is not frozen or waterlogged. Protect vulnerable plants like hebes and artemisias if frost is expected. Ensure stakes and ties on trees and climbers are firm against the wind. Order summer bulbs like gladioli for spring planting. Spray deciduous trees and shrubs with tar oil wash. Firm down roots of plants lifted by frost. Order alpine plants and pinks for spring planting. Keep dividing herbaceous plants when weather permits.

VEGETABLES, FRUIT AND HERBS

Continue planting fruit trees and bushes in good weather. Spray fruit trees and bushes with tar wash. Order vegetable seeds and seed potatoes. Spray peach trees against leaf curl with Bordeaux mixture or liquid copper. Apply a potash-based fertilizer to soft fruit. Sow broad beans (aquadilce) and lettuces such as Fortune under cloches. Plant rhubarb crowns and cover with manure. Apply a nitrogen-based fertilizer to fruit trees grown in grass.

PLANTS UNDER PROTECTION

Keep house-plants in light. Keep compost slightly moist. Make early sowings of alpine strawberries, onions and cauliflowers for planting out in April. Sow sweet pea seeds. Sow first tomatoes if heat is 60F (16C). Check pelargonium cuttings and throw out failures. Sow gloxinias and begonias if heat is 60–65F (16–18C). Bring in more bowls of bulbs from outdoors to force for the house. Ventilate greenhouse on warm days.

OTHER JOBS

Clean and sharpen garden tools. Keep aerating the lawn.

Winter colours

IN GARDENING TERMS, January really separates the men from the boys. Any amateur can have an attractive summer garden brimming with bedding plants which have been bought, half-grown, from the nursery. But to have a garden which looks delicious at this bleaker time of year requires a considerable amount of knowledge and planning.

In a town, where your garden is so much an extension of the house, it is doubly important that it should look pleasing now, with a variety of evergreens in varying shades of green, yellow and silver and with flowers and shrubs in bloom. Those clear crisp sunny mornings, when the frost begins to melt in the first rays of the sun and becomes glistening dew-drops on the juniper leaves, can be truly idyllic. In fact the colour schemes in winter can be infinitely more subtle than anything the summer could contrive.

A successful winter garden depends largely on leaves, and on the varied juxtaposition of one plant with another. However, there are certain plants and shrubs which flower now and since you will want to plant in March, after the heavy frosts, you might do some reconnoitring during this month. It's important of course to plant your winter flowers within close range of the house so they can still be admired from the warmth of your sitting room.

Particular favourites are the hellebores. *Helleborus niger*, the Christmas rose, is out now. The rest follow on and I have mentioned them in March. *Daphne mezeureum* is another delightful winter flowering shrub with her deliciously scented little mauve flowers which should appear any day. Another daphne which I value every bit as much is *Daphne odora* Aureomarginata. This is the evergreen form of daphne and has the added interest that the finely shaped, small thin leaves have a pale yellow margin. In late winter it will flower with the most fragrant pale purple blossoms. Daphnes do like to have a bit of sun so avoid a north-facing wall.

Mahonias, conversely, are happy in shade. They are those evergreen shrubs with holly-like leaves and long strands of tiny lemon-yellow flowers. *Mahonia* Charity is flowering now, producing the most spectacular flowers of all the mahonia family. They stick out at right angles to the stem in groups and are very sweetly scented, so one little snip added to a posy by your bed can be extraordinarily cheering. *M. japonica* will follow in February. Her flowers smell even sweeter but are less showy. In spring M. *aquifolium* will bear much thicker clusters of bright yellow flowers, which I love. The leaves may also give you the bonus of turning a reddish colour in winter. In the summer, these shrubs will still be valuable, providing as they do a rich, deep green background against which your summer flowers can shine.

If you have space, a witch hazel (*Hamamelis mollis*) looks captivating and flowers this month. It carries most unusual gold, frilly flowers on its branches and looks especially attractive when arranged in the house. But remember that it will spread to about ten feet, so give it space. Another cheering yellow is provided by forsythia – that gay bush which bears bright yellow star-like flowers in winter. The drooping variety *F. suspensa* has no objection to a north wall. Periwinkle (vinca) is a plant I have always loved. Those deep blue flowers always surprise you in summer when the plant has yet again trailed somewhere new, often into a darkish spot where no other plant would wish to live. But in winter the evergreen leaves have a quality all of their own and the variegated type is especially striking now.

All variegated leaves show up marvellously in the bright winter sunlight and also cheer a dull day. The most ravishing is *Elaeagnus pungens* Maculata. This is a slow-growing bush but even when quite small it cuts a dash with its vivid yellow leaves with green markings. The ordinary *E. pungens* is not variegated, but is worth growing for its fine silvery-green leaves with silver undersides. I use these a lot in flower arrangements and they never pall.

Fatsia japonica is an oddly un-English shrub with its large, bright, glossy seven-pointed leaves that resemble fig leaves. Many people grow it as a house plant, but it is hardy and evergreen and doesn't mind quite a lot of shade. Try one in a tub in a dark basement and you should not be disappointed. It is always striking in summer and can easily grow up to six feet (in Jersey I have seen them over twenty feet). But in December it comes into its own, lasting through this month with rather bizarre but fascinating green flowers. There is also a variegated form which should be in a lighter spot if its creamy markings are to keep.

Another shade-loving evergreen is *Garrya elliptica*. This will cheerfully climb up a north wall giving a fine show of silvery-green leaves. Just now it presents us with the most charming bunches of soft, greenish catkins which can also look delightful if cut and brought into the house.

Time to spray

At this time of year the last thing you probably want to do is go out to do wet, cold and rather dirty jobs. This surely is the time of planning? However, if you value your fruit crop you should be getting busy now. For now, while your fruit trees are sensibly dormant, is the time for three jobs: spraying, pruning and feeding. And the most important is spraying.

For fruit growers, life is one long battle against pests and disease. Professional growers may spray as many as ten times a year and an amateur, with an orchard at the bottom of the garden, should certainly spray three times. If, like many small gardeners, you have perhaps just an apple or two, a pear and a plum, then a winter tar wash now, followed by further spraying with insecticide such as Formothion or Dimethoate in early summer after the petals have fallen (you do not want to harm pollinating bees), is essential.

A tar wash kills aphids which are one of the biggest garden pests. They come in many varieties – there are six that attack currants alone. If your apple tree was infested by rosy apple aphid last year, (and it is very common) attack it now. This aphid clusters in thousands around the young shoots, giving out a sticky substance which causes the leaves to curl and the young fruit to drop. Just now the aphid eggs are overwintering on the pear, apple, plum, peach and cherry, as well as the cane fruits such as gooseberries, currants and raspberries. Go to your garden centre and ask for a tar oil winter wash – dilute it with water as instructed on the bottle.

A tar wash is strong stuff and you do not want it to harm neighbouring trees or flowers, or the grass below the tree you are spraying. Choose a frost-free time when there is as little wind as possible and lay old newspaper round the base of the tree to catch the drips. With large, old fruit trees you are limited in the amount of spraying you can do; but nowadays many fruit trees are dwarf varieties (grafted onto smaller stocks) which makes the fruit easier to pick. These, and medium-sized trees, can be tackled with a hand spray or, failing that, with the large two gallon sprays which you pump.

It is difficult to write about pruning without being able to demonstrate, and it is a subject that confuses people. The whole purpose of pruning fruit trees is to keep them in good shape, which in the case of cordons and espaliers is so important. It is also intended to get rid of the dead and weak branches. Most fruit trees you buy in garden centres are two or three years old and have already been pruned back to encourage the shaping process. If your young tree has, say, three or four branches you will, but cutting them back by two thirds, double your branches next year. But remember, it will not harm your tree to leave it unpruned. With all pruning the message is: if in doubt, don't.

Finally, fruit trees must be fed, particularly when they are young. I get an annual visit from the manure seller and spread his wares liberally around the base of my trees. Even if your trees are in an orchard, it is sensible to leave some bare soil around the base of the tree so that you can feed it well in its early years. A good dose of manure or rich compost in the next month or so should pay dividends later.

Bulbs for summer

Amaryllis, agapanthus, alstroemeria and acidanthera. These are just a few of the glorious summer bulbs which could grace your garden and, like their names, add more than a touch of the exotic. I mention this, for now is the time to order them if you want to do that spring planting. It is also the time to plan your summer border – ordering new herbaceous plants to plant out in March as the weather improves.

Summer bulbs and tubers, while popular, are nowhere near as much in demand as spring ones. This, I suppose, is because there are so many gay bedding plants to catch the eye in June. But some bulbs and tubers proliferate – few suburban gardens feel complete without their gladioli and dahlias in late summer and begonias are popular, if only for their sheer staying power, though I have to admit that begonias and I have never really hit it off. To my mind there are a host of much more beautiful summer bulbs which you could, and should, try.

Mark you, summer bulbs do not come cheaply. Lilies may look expensive, but they are bargain basement compared to agapanthus – those exquisite tall plants from South Africa with a huge, round cluster of brilliant blue or white flowers on the end of a long, erect stem. What is more, agapanthus look silly on their own, rather as a tall tulip does, and must be planted in groups: so up goes the bill. In South Africa they line the roadside like so many weeds, but here they need more care. I treat myself to a few more each year and in late November divide up some of my old ones. This way I am increasing the stock and by now have quite an impressive group in ravishing colours, from white through lighter blues to deep, gentian blue.

So, despite the expense, summer bulbs, if given attention and fed regularly, will pay you back by going on from year to year and multiplying with gusto. Don't be tempted to buy inferior bulbs because they seem cheap. A reputable firm (see Appendix VI) will supply them quite reasonably (probably more reasonably than your local garden centre), give you a much wider choice and prove a better investment in the long term.

Most summer bulbs should be planted around March, and the more tender ones like ixia (the corn lily), begonias and dahlias when the frosts have gone. Lilies, however, can be planted from January whenever the ground is not frosted or waterlogged. With few exceptions all bulbs need good drainage if they are not to rot. So when you plant (near the surface for agapanthus and begonias, at about five inches down for the rest) remember to dig the ground well, incorporating a lot of peat and humus before you get started.

As bulbs have their own food supply they tend to need less feeding than, say, bedding plants. As usual, there are exceptions. Gladioli, agapanthus and dahlias need all they can get if they are to flower as well next year. It's a good idea to spread a good handful of bonemeal (a long-lasting fertilizer) when planting any bulbs and to give the heavy feeders regular doses of fertilizer in summer and a good mulch or compost in winter.

Some bulbs of which I am becoming increasingly fond are alliums. These are part of the onion family and their general appearance is of a great round ball of fluffy mauve, white or purple flowers balanced, surprisingly, on the end of a tall, erect stem. If you have space at the back of a border, a group of *Allium giganteum* with their mauve heads attracting all the bees, will grow to four feet and last through July. *A. albopilosum* is similarly round-headed but has a very lacy head and only grows a foot tall. Little alliums that I have spreading around the garden are *A. neapolitanum* (daffodil garlic) which grows about a foot and has delicate heads of white flowers. It naturalizes very well in grass as does *A. moly luteum* which is similar and blooms bright yellow in June. With both of these, don't buy less than about twenty-five bulbs for a good clump – not so much of a hardship, since they are cheap.

In late summer when so many bright flowers are over, you will really appreciate *Amaryllis belladonna*. This rather delicate plant (put it in a sheltered sunny spot) grows about eighteen inches tall and bears a large cluster of soft rose-pink flowers in early September. They are really delicate and beautiful. I particularly love alstroemeria (Peruvian lily) which you so often see in florists as a cut flower but which will do fine in a clump in a sheltered spot. These are tall lily-like flowers which come in shades from orange through pink to white and all have a rather exciting deep saffron striped tongue.

For town gardeners or patio lovers there is also the plus that many bulbs do extremely well in tubs. Lilies are a classic example and agapanthus can look quite spectacular. Large gladioli and alstroemeria would look ridiculous, but smaller gladioli are fine and again last a good few weeks. I was once told that of all the different specialist horticultural societies (the rose societies, Alpine Society, etc.) by far the grandest was the Iris Society. This was because in order to really go in for irises you had to have a garden large enough to be able to devote a whole border or area of the garden to these flowers which only bloom for three weeks of the year. The rest of the year you would close off that bit. I refer to the tall bearded iris, by far the most common form of iris, which flowers in June; of course there are also the little spring-flowering iris bulbs and strange exceptions like the lovely winter-flowering *Iris unguicularis* and the – I think rather dull – Gladwin iris (*Iris foetidissima*) which has blue summer flowers, is evergreen (most irises die back in winter) and has interesting orange seeds in strange pods.

In fact you need no big border. A substantial clump of irises in a sunny spot will give you immense pleasure. If you are really clever you will plant some in blending colours, for they come in such an amazing variety. Kelways, the iris specialists (see Appendix VI) list over 150 and then another fifty or so May-flowering varieties which they have achieved through crosses between the tall bearded irises and dwarf varieties. The colours are so attractive, so subtle and so various that it's no wonder that iris lovers get obsessive. There is one deep velvety one called Black Ink which I have my eye on, but the softer colours in coral and lemon and pink, not to mention the startling whites and oranges, are quite thrilling.

Irises can be planted and transplanted (for you can increase them greatly by division) in early spring from February onwards. As long as they have full sunlight they are pretty unfussy, but a good manuring in autumn when the leaves die back will help them along greatly.

Test your seeds

January is a broody month. There you are with the spoils of your seed catalogue, all set to get propagating, but there's a snag. With the exception of broad beans and shallots, which you should be sowing later this month if the weather becomes mild and not too wet, it's too early to do much other than dig. However, there is nothing to stop you planning. And mark my words, once sowing time begins you will regret any lack of forethought. If you have a lot of last year's seeds left over, you can save money by using some of them. But this could be a dreadful waste if they did not germinate. So test them now.

Soft-skinned seeds like parsnips are not worth sowing. They have a life of twelve months at the most. Beetroot, onion and carrot seeds are also temperamental. Most other vegetable seeds have a life of two to three years, and brassicas – cabbage, sprouts, broccoli etc. – can keep for seven years if kept in ideal conditions, i.e. a place both cool and dry. Damp is a seed's worst enemy for it can begin to germinate and then rot. It also dries out if kept too warm.

Take a saucer and line it with moistened blotting paper. Place, say, ten or twelve seeds of a given type on the paper, cover it with cling foil or polythene to ensure that no moisture is lost and then put the saucer somewhere warm like the airing cupboard ($60°$ F is about the right temperature). If in two to three weeks the seeds have made no sign of movement then throw away the parent pack. If over half have germinated then you are well away, as most people sow too thickly in the first place. Seed merchants generally expect an average of eighty per cent germination from their seeds. To me the great advantage of using last year's seeds is that I buy new varieties of, say, lettuce or tomato each year and so I can grow several kinds at once.

Easy house-plants

To keep healthy house-plants which you will so appreciate at this time of year you need to give them full-time attention. They should be kept moist, sprayed and fed in spring and summer, not allowed to get dusty or draughty, and re-potted at least once a year. This explains why my home is no haven for house-plants. It is something I regret, but from spring to late autumn I'm so preoccupied with the garden outside that they hardly get a look in. Only in the bleak dark months do they get the attention they deserve. This is a shaming admission, but it does make me quite an expert on the kind of house-plant which will muddle through gamely, despite gross neglect.

Their four great enemies are dryness, lack of light, improper watering – either too much or too little – and draughts. Humidifiers go a long way to combat the first enemy. Failing these you can create a moisturizing system with a larger water-tight pot holder. Place a layer of pebbles on the bottom of a pot holder or jardinière and then pour water to nearly cover the pebbles. Balance your plant pot on top of the pebbles and the water will create a more humid atmosphere for the plant. You can extend this scheme to a self-watering system by putting a wick (an old shoe lace will do) in the bottom of the pot and trailing it in the water. Never let a plant sit with its bottom in the water itself or the compost will turn sour and the plant die.

Sturdy house-plants include grape ivy (*Rhoicissus rhomboidea*) and weeping fig (*Ficus benjamina*). Both are delightfully-shaped, elegant plants with hanging leaves. Tradescantias (often called wandering jew) are very popular and I can see why. They look charming in hanging baskets or cascading from shelves. I find that *Chamaedorea* – a rather solid-looking palm – grows very well in a quite gloomy spot. Luckily there are quite a lot of plants that are tolerant of very shady places, the obvious example being common ivy (*Hedera helix*). While the variegated forms will lose much of their colour in shade, the plain dark variety will romp away. In America, where they are so adventurous with their house-plants, I have seen delightful screens of ivy consisting of, say, five plants in one window box trained up a trellis.

Another vigorous climber which has put up with my neglect for years is kangaroo vine (*Cissus antarctica*). This is not unlike grape ivy but has a larger leaf. It is well tried for withstanding all manner of temperature fluctuations. As with all these plants it needs regular summer feeds and annual repotting and will look more attractive and be healthier if the leaves are kept clean and occasionally sprayed.

Kangaroo vine, grape ivy and tradescantia are all ideal for hanging baskets, trailing, as they do, so elegantly. So is the sweetheart vine (*Philodendron scandens*). This last is not technically a climber – it does not have the little clinging tendrils – but can be trained up a trellis. Its glossy heart-shaped leaves are very attractive and should at all costs be kept clean and shiny. I always think that hanging baskets – particularly those rather elegant, white, woven string ones – can look so magical when hung in front of a window. If the view outside is not too grand they create a diversion, but also add an exotic touch as the sun dapples through them.

Rather than have lots of fussy little plants in a room, I prefer a large specimen plant. Again the Americans have no qualms about filling their houses with trees. One of my favourites and a very tolerant friend is *Ficus benjamina*, or weeping fig. It is justly popular with its silvery white trunk, gently curving branches and many slender, dark green leaves. Other elegant palm-like plants are paradise palms (*Howea forsteriana*) which I associate strongly with Edwardian hotels. Similarly Edwardian in appearance is the parlour palm (*Chamaedorea elegans*) which makes a fine smaller specimen plant.

House-plants should not be restricted to your home. Visitors to my office tend to object when a large *Philodendron lacineatum* – with its huge, finely arching, deeply cut leaves – arches over from the bookcase and gently tickles their ears. However, my green fancies are mere trifles compared with the mammoth growths which grace the workplaces of Americans. New York offices are a riot of plants, and office conversation dwells heavily on the health of our potted friends. Many office workers sit banked by displays which put our occasional straggly spider plants to shame. Americans talk to, love and indulge their house-plants with the same zest we devote to our outdoor plants.

Of course the problem in the office is that you are away at the weekend and things may not always get watered in your absence. A cleaner may leave the blind up and your poor defenceless tree, sitting in front of a huge plate glass window, will wither and die.

I think that a more reliable scheme in the office – and certainly less messy – is to grow plants that are planted hydroponically, i.e. in water.

Hydroponics – the science of growing things in water – is not new to the horticultural world, but it has been much perfected recently and many commercial firms are beginning to grow tomatoes and other vegetables that way. A lot of house-plants are now sold in special containers where their roots cling to light porous, sterile clay granules which look perfectly pleasant and stand in water to which special feeding substances have been added. The plants seem to flourish that way and of course they keep wonderfully clean.

Finally, the safest and one of the most interesting ways of growing house-plants is in a sealed glass container called a terrarium. Lots of experiments have been conducted recently with these and there are no end of ways you can make terrariums using anything from bottles and fishtanks to glass constructions which become an elegant, plant-filled coffee table. Of course, terrariums are not new. Their ancestors were those firm features of every middle-class Victorian drawing roon: the fern or Wardian case – after the famous Doctor Ward who stunned the Great Exhibition with a bottled garden which had remained sealed for eighteen years and yet flourished. Smart fern cases thereafter tended to look like miniature Crystal Palaces.

For beginners, the simplest solution (an example of which I have on the bathroom window ledge) is the fish aquarium. Necessary ingredients are pebbles which form a one- or two-inch layer of drainage on the bottom, followed by some chips of charcoal to keep the soil sweet and then some soil – I suggest special house-plant compost. Separate the soil from the drainage with some porous but unrottable fabric – I cut up an old nylon petticoat.

And now the fun starts. Your objective is a woodland glade in miniature, so you will need, as well as plants, decorative stones and sticks. I used an easy mixture of maidenhair fern (adiantum), goose foot (syngonium), croton (codiaeum), wandering jew (tradescantia), desert privet (peperomia) and, to trail along the ground, that cluster of tiny leaves called mind-your-own-business (*Helxine soleirolii*). Once they were arranged and planted up and watered I decorated the ground with beautiful exotic shells I had brought back from Africa. On top of the aquarium you could place a piece of glass cut to size, but keep it out of direct sunlight or the whole thing will steam up.

Heavenly clematis

An exciting aspect of gardening is that affections are never constant. Out come the lilies and positively vamp you, so you have eyes for no other flower. Then some weeks later you are calling a particular rose your favourite flower while the lilies fade away, knowing that next year they will capture your heart in just the same way again. But the flower that constantly bewitches me is the clematis. There is something so delicate about these ravishing climbers in their soft shades of pink and white ranging to deep, velvet lavender, that you feel a breeze could lift them away. In fact they are marvellously sturdy, carrying on valiantly from year to year – and this makes you love them even more.

Some people make the mistake of growing clematis alone against a wall, although another appealing aspect of their character is that they are immensely friendly and will climb up any other shrub without complaint (but give the shrub a few years to get established first). This makes them perfect for small gardens as they use comparatively little space. It also gives you wonderful scope for experiment. Grow a late summer-flowering clematis up a June-flowering ceanothus and you have a good succession of colour. Or go for the big effect and plan a purple C. *jackmanii* on a yellow rose like Mermaid which will bloom simultaneously.

We have been growing clematis in our gardens ever since C. *viticella* was introduced from Spain and named Virgin's Bower after Queen Elizabeth I. Our native clematis is, of course, the C. *vitalba* of the hedgerows, known to all as old man's beard. A visit to the Chelsea Flower Show in May gives a taste of the enormous variety available. There are several excellent specialist firms (see Appendix VI) which come out in style there, displaying banks of huge breathtaking star-like flowers.

As clematis are pot-grown you can plant them any time. But now (making sure the ground is not frosty or waterlogged when you plant) is as good a time as any as the plants are still dormant and can get established before producing shoots. Clematis are pretty unfussy about soil but they need to be kept moist in the first year or so, so don't plant them too close to the wall where it is dryest. It is best to try and keep their roots in the shade and some people lay flat stones or tiles on the ground around the plant once it is installed and well-watered to try and eliminate the chance of it drying out.

I grow lots of clematis which gives me colour from May until the autumn. They are, in order of appearance: *C. montana rubens*; Vyvyan Pennell which is a most unusual double violet blue and reappears in the autumn with single flowers; *C. henryi* with the largest single white flowers in mid-summer; Comtesse de Bouchaud which is a lovely single rose-coloured variety flowering for months; good old *jackmanii* growing up an Albertine rose (Albertine flowers in early summer only so this takes over) and vivid wine-red Ernest Markham. Of these the only mistake was *C. montana rubens*, for though it quite intoxicates you in May, it grows at such a rate that I spend my whole time cutting it back. However, if you have a shed to cover it is the plant for you.

Another heavenly spring-flowering clematis is *C. armandii* with its mass of small star-like white flowers and good foliage which also has the bonus of being evergreen. I would also recommend *C. alpina* whose soft blue flowers are distinguished by their nodding, Chinese-lantern shapes. Autumn-flowering *C. orientalis*, one of my favourites, also has Chinese-lantern flowers. It comes from Tibet and, in contrast to the pinks and mauves you expect, its hundreds of flowers are a vivid orange-yellow. They later form pretty fluffy heads like our native clematis. No wonder our ancestors called our own clematis traveller's joy.

FEBRUARY

FLOWERS, SHRUBS AND TREES

Prune shrubs which flower on this year's wood, like buddleias and fuchsias, back to about 12 in. from the base. Keep planting trees, shrubs and roses. Prune your clematis: those which bloom in high summer down to about 3 ft. from the base, but earlier flowering hybrids less severely. Firm soil around plants dislodged by frost. Clear, weed and feed your herbaceous border. Keep planting lily bulbs. When snowdrops, helebores etc. finish flowering divide the clumps. Apply manure or compost to tubs containing permanent shrubs and plants.

VEGETABLES, FRUIT AND HERBS

Sow lettuces and cabbages under cloches. Sow broad beans and onions outdoors in fine weather. Plant Jerusalem artichokes. Complete pruning of apples, pears and bush fruits. Keep planting fruit trees and bushes. Spray peaches and nectarines against leaf curl. Keep spraying fruit trees with tar oil before buds open. Prepare your runner bean bed by working in lots of manure or compost. Place seed potatoes in trays in an airy, frost-free place. Prune autumn fruiting raspberries and cut back newly planted canes to about 10 in. Start to scatter slug pellets. Sow parsley in good weather.

PLANTS UNDER PROTECTION

Sow seeds of petunias, geraniums, antirrhinums in slight heat. Sow tomato and wild strawberry seeds in slight heat. Start off begonias and gloxinias in compost. Fumigate or spray the greenhouse if necessary. Aerate as much as possible on fine days. Bring in bowls of bulbs from your garden plunge bed to force for the house. Repot large house plants, removing dead roots and placing in larger pots with fresh compost.

LAWNS

Prepare ground for lawn sowing. Dig and remove weeds. Aerate established lawns. Check for moss and scarify.

Seed sowing

I HAVE ALWAYS dreaded February. It is sometime during this month that you feel that winter is never, never going to end. The occasional day will dawn cheerful and you will be tempted out into the garden only to be defeated by the ground being too frosty or by a sudden fall of snow or rain. If you are thus thwarted you can give your morale a bit of a boost with thoughts for the summer – even if it does seem it will never come – and get sowing a few seeds in warmth under glass.

Being a Yorkshire lass there's nothing I hate more than waste, and few things strike me as more wasteful – and lazy for that matter – than buying fully-grown annuals. After all, those petunias or mari-golds for the window box could easily be grown from seed for a fraction of the cost. Why is it then that every June, garden centres do a roaring trade in petunias, geraniums, marigolds etc., all at vast prices when with a bit of foresight the buyers could have the huge satisfaction of growing them from seed? I can only imagine they've no idea how easy it is. Everyone knows it's simple to grow a row of carrots directly in the soil. However, the idea of forcing plants under glass indoors puts people off. But don't be alarmed, it's like falling off a log. You won't need a heated greenhouse, only your warm, light window ledge. Add to that a few seed trays, seed and potting compost, a packet of seeds and you're off.

If you have a greenhouse you might also think of investing in an electric propagator for it. It will use much less electricity than heating the whole place, but will provide bottom-heat and protection from the frosty air. There are a good many on the market, so nose around in your local garden centre.

Nothing looks prettier than a mass of petunias flowering in a window box from June to October and there are dazzling colours and variations to choose from. I always grow white ones. One year it was Snowdrift, a lovely F1 hybrid from Suttons. Another year I chose the larger flowered White Cascade from Unwins.

If you start this month with petunias, geraniums, antirrhinums or begonias you will have banks of flowers in June for very little investment, when your neighbours are paying sky-high prices. First buy some seed compost (I prefer the crumbly John Innes sort to the peat-based ones). Lay newspaper thickly on your kitchen table and place beside it a plastic tub containing two inches of water. Fill your seed tray with compost, firm it down and dampen it by placing the tray in your water tub (don't do this in the sink or you might block the drain). Allow it to drain on the newspaper, then sow the seeds thinly.

Newly sown seeds need be barely covered. When you prick out, hold the seedling gently by its leaves. Avoid touching the stem.

Petunia and geranium seeds are so tiny they barely need covering. Just sieve a sprinkling of compost over them, then cover the seed tray with more newspaper and place on the window sill. Once the seeds begin to sprout, remove the newspaper and put the plastic propagator lid on (you need not use one of these, but it does speed growing and stops the earth drying). Water them, gently testing the soil with your finger before doing so, until the seedlings look quite sturdy and have about four leaves. At this point you can prick them out using something like a small knife or dibber, always handling the seedlings gently by the leaves and not touching the stems or tiny roots. Transplant them into trays of potting compost, about two inches apart, or into individual little pots.

Then the answer is to just keep watering gently and put them in as light a place as possible, though not in a sunny spot where they might wither. They will have to be transplanted again in late spring when they begin to get crowded and you want to stop the plants getting too leggy. This is a tricky time for it is when you still cannot plant tender plants outdoors and space gets scarce. This is when a greenhouse with a little bit of heat can help a good deal.

At the end of this month sow tomatoes, cucumbers and peppers, annual and everlasting sweet peas, morning glory for your trellis, nicotiana and lovely lavatera (or mallow). Try the marvellous white *Lavatera* Mont Blanc and the other new introduction Silver Cup which is a glorious soft pink. Late February is also a good time to get lettuce seedlings like Tom Thumb and Little Gem going to sow outdoors at Eastertime, so that they come out in succession. Antirrhinums, French marigolds, alyssum and lobelia, *Cobaea scandens* that lovely purple climber, impatiens (busy lizzie), pansies and the lovely annual *Phlox drummondii* will all benefit from a start now.

Reflective pools

If this year you feel the need for a new project, why not think of a garden pool? Just about now you can start dreaming of the exotic water plants like irises and water lilies to place there in May along with all sorts of fish and those flowers you can plant around the pool which will create stunning effects with their reflections.

There was a time when laying a garden pool in concrete (which tended to crack and leak) was a real palaver. But the days of PVC and glass fibre have put an end to that. Laying a pond is comparatively straightforward these days and now is a good time to start preparing. You want to have it complete by April in order to install your water plants.

A pool can make such a difference to a small London garden if it is well planned and can fit in with the whole scheme. It acts as an interesting focal point but also gives a feeling of calm and placidity in contrast to the floral activity around. Siting is important. Avoid anywhere that is overhung by trees, or the leaves will fall into the pond and rot. Water plants need sun, so your spot must have sunlight for at least half the day during the summer.

Having chosen your site, decide on the shape and size. If you have money to spare you might investigate what glass fibre pools your garden centre has to sell. But it's cheaper and more fun to create your own shape and line it with Butyl rubber or PVC, which a garden centre or a specialist company will stock. Both are expected to last a hundred years, and enough for a pool seven feet by five feet should not cost an enormous amount. The pond should be around eighteen inches deep but have more shallow shelves: say, eight inches deep around the edge for plants which need less depth. When working out the PVC length remember you will need an extra six inches around the edge of the pond, just overhanging the lip, which you can conceal with stones. Unfold the liner over your newly-dug pool, weighting the edges with stones. Run a little water in and shape the liner round as you fill it completely.

Water lilies (nymphaea) are a must. When making your choice I recommend a booklet called *Water Gardens*, from the Royal Horticultural Society. Some varieties would suit only lakes whereas others like my old favourite the crimson N. Froebellii or rose pink James Brydon are ideal for smaller pools. Another charming pink is Rose Arey. I particularly love the yellow varieties like soft-coloured *N. x marliacea* Chromatella. All these flower best in water between nine and twenty-four inches deep. But there are also beautiful miniatures which can be planted on the shallower ledges near the pool edge, like tiny white N. *pygmaea*. The easiest way to plant lilies and the other water plants is in special plastic water baskets with holes round the sides. Line the baskets with hessian or cotton

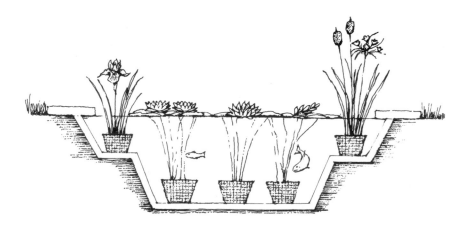

(I use an old shirt), plant them firmly using good garden soil, throwing in some bonemeal to set them off right and cover the surface with pebbles. Soak the basket in water before putting it in the pool and then place it on the pool floor, wedging it with large stones until it roots.

Irises look charming on the pool edge, but do be sure to buy ones that will not grow too tall and hide other plants. *Iris laevigata* which grows to around one and a half feet and blooms in many colours, sometimes with variegated leaves, is ideal. Water hawthorn (*Aponogeton distachyum*) is another popular and reliable plant. Its white flowers float on the surface of the water in all seasons and have a sweet scent.

Finally, no pond is complete without fish. The suppliers of pond liners and plants also stock fish. A big favourite nowadays is Japanese Koi carp, but as you can get about a dozen goldfish for the price of one carp, I should start off with them.

Don't forget the potatoes

Historically, potato crops have been fickle and they remain so to this day. If one year is dry, then the following year will bring high prices for potatoes and everyone will become anxious about shortages. I remember one day in early February when my boss called me on the internal 'phone demanding to see me pronto. I feared the worst. Certainly he looked as desperate as he sounded. He came straight to the point. 'Where,' said he in a tone of near frenzy, 'can I find seed potatoes?' That year, after a hot summer, the crop was late and small.

Even if prices are high I think it's worth growing a row or two for there is nothing tastier than your own potatoes, and seed potatoes should be in the shops just now.

Unless you have acres of space, it's not worth growing the later maincrop potatoes. New ones use less space and can also be grown – wait for it – in tubs. If, like me, you just want two short rows and a few tubs you might consider splitting a three kilo bag with a friend. Your shop may stock three or more varieties. I like Home Guard and Pentland Javelin. Other popular ones are Arran Pilot, Sharpe's Express, Ulster Sceptre and Epicure. When they arrive, place your potatoes in a dry, shallow box in a light, frost-free place. Then wait for them to sprout. They may produce many sprouts, but you should cut these down to three strong ones and wait to plant out around mid-March. Dig a trench six inches deep and place the potatoes about twelve inches apart. Then cover them up and apply a fertilizer such as Growmore or Phostrogen. As shoots appear, cover them with earth – this is called 'earthing up' – to keep off the frost. The potatoes should be ready in June.

Now for the fun. With a greenhouse, or sunny window ledge for that matter, you can force potatoes in tubs later this month. Plant a couple of sprouting potatoes in a ten-inch pot using a mixture of John Innes No 3 and peat. Water regularly and when the shoots appear feed the plant with some fertilizer – Phostrogen for example – every fortnight or so. This way you should have quite a crop in May.

Tactful climbers

My first London house – typical of many thousands with two-up-two-down and a narrow garden at the back – had only one snag: the garden with its three-foot walls gave no privacy. While riveted by the street gossip from the neighbour on my left as we pruned, I longed for a bit of fence. But how could I build a fence without seeming unfriendly? It was my Greek neighbour on the right who provided the clue – by high summer he had disappeared from view behind a wall of giant dahlias. I decided that I too would grow some privacy – and I did.

Climbing plants can transform a garden. Your whole level of vision changes. Few things look lovelier than banks of clematis and honeysuckle in summer and glowing red pyracantha in autumn. February and March are good months for planting. Before embarking, get your supports firmly fixed. The attractive diamond-shaped wooden-latticed fencing available at garden centres is good for a sheltered garden. My garden was not sheltered and my first effort blew down in a gale. For windy gardens you want something the wind blows through; I decided on plastic-coated netting – less attractive but soon concealed; it has survived attached to metal stakes dug into the ground and fastened to the wall. It made the garden look like a small tennis court at first but was soon covered with plants. When planting, remember that soil near the base of a wall is generally poor and a specimen planted there will get little water. So if possible plant about eighteen inches out. Dig a large hole two feet wide and fill it with good compost and rotted manure.

When I first saw a mauve wisteria flowering in a yellow laburnum tree I realized just how boundless is the potential of climbers. Some people miss half the point, thinking of them only as wall plants, but an imaginative gardener can get them to do no end of things – climb over pergolas of all styles and shapes, bridges, trees – in fact over anything. What is more – and here is the scope for subtle or bizarre colour combinations – they can climb up each other. And on a more mundane level, they are an effective disguise for those parts of your house and garden which you like least. For those who live in town, with a pocket-handkerchief garden, climbers are particularly important, as they make use of the vertical space outside your house.

There are three kinds of climbers: the clingers, the twiners and the leaners. The clingers are those such as ivy, Virginia creeper, and the glorious white *Hydrangea petiolaris* which actually have little pads on their stems with which they attach themselves to the wall. They are best placed against something solid like a wall or fence, but will happily make their way up trees. The twiners hold on to whatever they climb, either with delicate but tenacious tendrils, as in the case of the passion flower and the sweet pea, or with the stems of their leaves or flowers, as in the case of the clematis and the honeysuckle. In the wild, the ancestors of the twiners grew up trees or in the hedge-rows; so these, if not too voracious, are good candidates for attaching themselves to more solid climbers such as mature roses. Finally, the leaners are really shrubs which grow upwards with no clinging mechanism, so they must be trained. They include roses, powdery blue ceanothus, red or yellow-berried pyracantha and wisteria. Wisteria takes time to get going but will repay your patience a hundredfold.

Almost anything will thrive against a south-facing wall. Some roses, such as Madame Grégoire Staechelin, are suggested for north-facing walls, but don't expect them to bloom in as much profusion as they would if they were in full sun. On the other hand, there are plants such as *H. petiolaris*, evergreen pyracantha and Virginia creeper which seem not to know the difference. I am especially fond of the butter-coloured kerria which flowers cheerily in April on my north wall along with the daffodils

Some other good bets for shade are the enchanting spring-flowering shrub Japanese quince (chaenomeles), which blooms in scarlet, pink or white; *Garrya elliptica*, which has the advantage of being both evergreen and producing its yellow-green catkins in the depth of winter when there is little else to cheer; in addition, all kinds of ivy and the *Clematis jackmanii* and *montana*, will tolerate shade.

I am particularly fond of climbing roses, and here the choice is breathtaking. A visit to one of the old formal French rose gardens, such as Roseraie de L'Hay-les-Roses (see July), is a great education in how pergolas and screens can be used to good effect. One finds there mostly old-fashioned ramblers like the rich, rose-pink Dorothy Perkins and Wedding Day with its mass of little open white flowers. The snag with these is that they only flower in high summer. Most more modern roses will blossom again in the autumn, so it makes sense to choose at least some of them. However, a rose such as corally pink Albertine will reward you with so many blooms in June that you will forgive her non-appearance later.

A really faithful rose is Mermaid, with enchanting, single canary-yellow flowers; it blossoms from June right through to October. There is something strangely innocent about those open blooms. The colour is fine against both brick and stone, and somehow always combines well with other flowers. Not dissimilar in the shape of its flower is Meg, a marvellously sturdy climber. The flowers are apricot pink and come out in summer and autumn. It is not a rose you see much, which is a pity. We grew soft, shell-pink New Dawn round our porch in my childhood, and its apple-like scent always evokes memories. It will flower in profusion all summer and enchant you. Not surprisingly it's still very popular.

To get an idea of the full scope of climbing roses, visit the Royal National Rose Society's gardens at Chiswell Green Lane, St Albans, Hertfordshire in July. It was there I first fell for a fine crimson-flowered Parkdirektor Riggers. It has glossy foliage and flowers continually in summer. Zephirine Drouhin is another favourite. It flowers surprisingly early, producing vivid carmine pink double flowers which reappear intermittently throughout the summer. Finally one modern rose which delights me is Pink Perpetua, with its lovely clear pink double blooms. (See Appendix VI for nurseries and catalogues.)

Clematis seems a natural bedmate for roses. While it would be a mistake to train the truly rampant *montana* up a rose (a good-sized tree is more its match) most clematis look more natural climbing up and around some other plant rather than straight against a wall, as one so often sees them (see January).

For instant privacy you could go for fast climbers like Russian vine or a fast growing honeysuckle like *Lonicera americana*. The snag here is that they don't know when to stop and you may spend year after year cutting them back. Better to plant marginally slower growers and fill the gap this year with annual climbers like sweet peas, morning glory (ipomoea), or *Cobaea scandens*.

Feed your soil

One of the few cheering aspects of February is the arrival at my doorstep of Mr Williams the manure man. Every winter he trundles his truckloads of rich, rotted horse manure up from Tooting and round the backstreets of north London. In past years I used to wait on tenterhooks for his call, but then I got more canny and took his address. So now I drop him a card saying how much I shall want and he dumps it whether I am there or not. There are people like Mr Williams all over the country and once you get to know them you have a tonic for your worn-out garden in need of all the feed it can get. For very little outlay you have enough manure to give the soil in your borders or vegetable patch the extra fillip it needs. For the manure not only adds all those nutrients your plants require if they are to flourish, but it also transforms the texture of the soil, providing humus which improves the drainage so that plants can breathe better and their roots grow more easily.

Now is a good time to spread manure and really dig it in (on days when the ground is not frozen stiff of course) so that it will have weathered and settled for spring sowing. If you have a vegetable patch you should go through this digging and spreading process every year, turning over the soil to about a spade's depth.

You cannot dig so deeply on borders without disturbing plants, but a surface spread lightly and turned into the soil should be enough. Deep digging with manure or compost is also essential if you are preparing ground to plant long-term occupants like trees and shrubs. Good garden compost is, of course, just as beneficial.

But in the average London garden you cannot make enough for your needs. Alternatively, there is the more expensive option of buying commercial composts and manures from garden centres. Whichever compost you choose, it is time to be putting in that investment which will only be realized when high summer arrives. A good manageable soil or loam should contain about equal parts of clay, gritty sand and humus, and all kinds of nutrients and trace elements which are essential to your plants' growth. The chief requirement is nitrogen which is what makes the leaves grow and flourish. Phosphorus and potassium are the other major essentials.

Hebes

Have you ever thought of having a hebe bed? I now have one and cannot tell you how interesting it is. I woke up to the variety of hebes when I first saw the stand of the County Park Nursery (see Appendix VI) at a Royal Horticultural Society show. This nursery specializes in these interesting evergreen shrubs from New Zealand whose flowers bloom in clusters of long spikes in white, pink, mauve or purple, like tiny buddleias; it lists well over 250 in its catalogue. I had no idea the choice was so large, for the average garden centre often has only five or six. They range from the very small varieties like Bowles' Hybrid which makes a charming little bush ideal for a rock garden and produces its soft lavender blooms all summer, to big bushes like Alicia Amherst with its vivid glossy leaves and strong purple spokes of flowers later in the summer.

Hebes come in many variegated forms such as the popular small *H. andersonii* which features in many town bedding schemes and is excellent in window boxes; they also come in silver-grey such as the dear *H.* Pagei which has charming white flowers and is ideal for ground cover. They are becoming more and more popular now for they have so many good points: they are evergreen; they don't mind being in light shade; they retain moisture in their thick leaves so are good for tubs; they are pretty unfussy about soil and the atmosphere in towns, and they grow quite fast as well as being extremely easy to propagate from cuttings. If you have not had much success taking other shrub cuttings, raise your morale and try with the hebe for it could not be easier.

[168]

The snag with some of them is that, coming as they do from the milder climate of New Zealand, certain varieties can get killed if you have a really hard winter when the frost continues for a long period without letting up. This is why I have my smaller hebes all in one place. About now when the frosts might do them in I put sacking or newspaper over them at night just in case. Wait to plant hebes till the spring. Then, if you are wise, you will take lots of cuttings in summer and keep these in the greenhouse or on a window ledge so that you always have replacements if you suffer losses.

In my little bed I have planted a cluster of three small varieties which all blend together as they all have dark green leaves and spikes in different graduations from mauve to purple throughout the summer. These are Bowles' Hybrid. Walter Buccleugh and Caledonia. Then there is contrasting *H*. Pagei, which forms a nice silver background. In total contrast again is *H. macrantha* which is also tiny but has bright yellowy green foliage and amazing large white flowers which are specially attractive.

Behind them grows *H*. Gauntlettii which will grow much larger to perhaps three feet and have merry pink flowers. Nearby is my favourite *H. franciscana* Variegata. The variegations on this beautiful shrub are so subtle – just as if you had taken to your green leaves a water colour brush, dipped in a silver-cream wash. It will also grow to two or three feet and have the bonus of pleasant mauvy-blue flowers.

For a cheering sight, as the rest of the gardens begins to lose heart, try autumn glory. It makes a compact and pleasantly rounded shrub eventually reaching around two feet in height. Its foliage is a very pleasant backdrop all summer. Later, out come those really royal purple flowers – hundreds of them – which I find quite spellbinding.

APPENDIX I

Some useful shrubs and plants for shady spots

SHRUBS

Aucuba japonica (Spotted laurel)
Camellia japonica
Camellia x williamsii Donation
Chaenomeles speciosa (Japanese quince)
Choisya ternata (Mexican orange blossom)
Clematis montana
Cornus canadensis (Creeping dogwood)
Euonymus fortunei radicans Variegatus
Fatsia japonica (Caster oil plant)
Garrya elliptica
Hedera helix (Common ivy)
Hydrangea petiolaris (Climbing hydrangea)
Hypericum calycinum (Rose of Sharon)
Ilex aquifolium (Holly)
Jasminum nudiflorum (Winter jasmine)

Lonicera japonica halliana (Japanese honeysuckle)
Mahonia aquifolium
Polygonum baldschuanicum (Russian vine)
Prunus laurocerasus (Cherry laurel)
Pyracantha (Firethorn)
Rhododendron
Roses:
    Danse du Feu
    Gloire de Dijon
    Iceberg
    Mme Alfred Carrière
    Mme Grégoire Staechelin
    Maigold
    Mermaid
    Parkdirektor Riggers
Skimmia japonica
Viburnum tinus
Vinca major (Greater periwinkle)
Vinca minor (Lesser periwinkle)

PLANTS

Ajuga reptans (Bugle)
Alchemilla mollis (Lady's mantle)
Anemone nemorosa (Wood anemone)
Aquilegia (Columbine)
Asperula odorata (Sweet woodruff)
Bergenia (Elephants' ears)
Campanula
Convallaria majalis (Lily-of-the-valley)
Digitalis purpurea (Foxglove)
Euphorbia wulfenii (Spurge)
Geranium grandiflorum

Helleborus atrorubens (Hellebore)
  H. corsicus
  H. niger (Christmas rose)
  H. orientalis (Lenten rose)
Hosta
Lamium galeobdolon (Yellow archangel)
Paeonia (Peony)
Polygonatum multiflorum (Solomon's seal)
Primula
Viola cornuta

APPENDIX II

Some plants for window boxes and small tubs

As with shrubs, many flowers can grow happily in containers as long as they are watered regularly and fed with liquid feed and longlasting fertilizers; these are some I have tried with success.

Agapanthus. In blue or white. Striking African lily.
Alyssum. Excellent edging plant, white.
Alchemilla. Frothy green flowered lady's mantle.
Antirrhinum. Excellent. Flowers all summer long.
Arabis. To tumble over the edge of larger tubs.
Artemisia. Many varieties of this silver-leafed plant, which is generally very draught-proof.
Aubrieta. Purple flowers forming large clumps. Ideal for hanging over the side of larger tubs.
Begonia. Many vivid coloured varieties.
Campanula. Small varieties are good for edging bigger tubs.
Chionodoxa. Lovely spring bulbs ideal for window boxes.
Chrysanthemum. Grow compact spray varieties.
Cobaea scandens. Blue-flowered annual climber.
Crocus. Dutch varieties good for tubs.
Dahlia. Choose shorter varieties for tubs.
Dianthus. Small pinks good for window boxes.
Fuchsia.
Geranium. (See *Pelargonium*).
Impatiens holstii. Busy Lizzie. Long flowering in window boxes.
Ipomoea. Morning glory. Grows along a trellis.
Iris reticulata. For window boxes.
Lilium. All varieties excellent.
Lobelia. Tiny blue or white cascading flowers.
Marigold. African and French excellent and long flowering.
Muscari. Bright blue grape hyacinths.
Nasturtium. Need sun, thrive on neglect.
Narcissus. All kinds of daffodil thrive in tubs.
Nicotiana. Tobacco plant. Long flowering and sweet smelling.
Pansy and *Viola*. Long flowering.
Pelargonium. Ivy leaved varieties particularly lovely. All ideal for containers.
Petunia. Cascades flowering all summer.
Polyanthus. Do need regular water or will die.
Senecio cineraria. Fine silver-leaved plant.

Sweet Pea. Short forms for window boxes, train others along trellis.
Tulip. Use short varieties and species like *T. tarda*.
Wallflower. Green leaves cheer tubs in winter. Flowers May–June.
  Choose short varieties.

APPENDIX III

Some trees and shrubs suitable for tubs

Almost anything can grow in a tub, but the following list I have grown
myself or seen grow happily in friends' tubs. As tubs generally stand close
to the house always in view they are selected for all-year interest and
also for draught resistance. . . . But remember tubs needs regular watering –
daily in hot summer – and feeding.

Acer dissectum. Elegant slow-growing maple.
Buddleia. Butterfly bush. Grows fast, needs annual prune.
Buxus sempervirens. Common box for screening.
Camellia. Spring flowers and wonderful evergreen leaves. Needs much
  water.
Chamaecyparis Pygmaea Argentea. Small bluish slow-growing cypress.
Choisya ternata. Evergreen with white flowers. Protect from wind.
Clematis. For training up walls or pergolas. Keep roots in shade.
Daphne odora. Evergreen with fragrant February flowers.
Elaeagnus pungens Maculata. Brilliant yellow variegated evergreen.
Eucalyptus gunnii. Unusual silver leaves. Prune hard in April to stop it
  becoming a tall tree.
Euonymus fortunei. Creeping variegated evergreen.
Fatsia japonica. Very striking evergreen. Good in shade.
Hebe. Many varieties and sizes, but most evergreen and excellent in
  draught.
Hedera helix. Ivy is very draught resistant.
Juniperus virginiana Skyrocket. Grey-blue evergreen. Striking upright
  shape.
Lavandula. Good evergreen grey foliage. Needs sun.
Lonicera. Honeysuckle. Evergreen varieties. Ideal for patio walls.
Pernettya. Evergreen shrub with pink or white berries in winter.
Pieris formosa forrestii. Brilliant red leaves and white flowers. Hates
  lime.
Potentilla. Shrubby shape with many flowers produced June to October.

Rhododendron and azalea. Go for small varieties. Use lime-free soil
and water copiously.

Roses. Most climbing roses are fine in tubs as are long-flowering
floribundas like Iceberg.

Ruta. Blue rue is a striking evergreen making fine clumps.

Salvia officinalis. Sage in various leaf colours makes elegant clumps.

Santolina. Silver cotton lavender is very draught resistant. Must be
pruned to keep shape.

Senecio greyi. Silver evergreen leaves. Very draught resistant and useful.

Viburnum tinus. Pretty-shaped dark, glossy evergreen with white flowers.

Wisteria. Can grow happily in a deep tub.

Yucca. Excellent architectural shape of evergreen rosette leaves makes
them ideal tub plants.

APPENDIX IV

Ground cover plants

Alchemilla mollis. Lady's mantle.
Anthemis cupaniana.
Anthemis nobilis.
Arabis.
Artemisia canescens
Alyssum saxatilis.
Calluna vulgaris. Heather, Ling
Campanula
Campanula poscharskyana.
Convolvulus cneorum
Dianthus. Garden pinks.
Erica carnea. Heather.
Erigeron.
Euonymus.
Euphorbia epithymoides
    (polychroma). Spurge.
Geranium endressii
Geranium macrorrhizum.
Hebe pinguifolia Pagei.
Hedera canariensis Azorica.
Hedera helix. Common ivy.
Helianthemum. Rock roses.
Helleborus. Christmas and Lenten
    roses.

Hosta
Hypericum calycinum. St John's
    wort.
Iberis sempervirens. Candytuft.
Lamium maculatum.
Lavandula. Lavender.
Nepeta faassenii. Cat mint.
Origanum vulgare Aureum.
    Marjoram.
Potentilla.
Pulmonaria.
Ruta. Blue rue.
Salvia officinalis. Common sage
Santolina. Cotton lavender.
Saxifrage hybrids.
Sedum.
Stachys clanata.
Thymus serpyllum.
Vinca minor. Lesser periwinkle.
Viola conuta.
Viola species.

APPENDIX V

Your gardening library

As your enthusiasm grows you will want to read and learn more. So here is a list of gardening books I would not like to be without.

The Well-Tempered Garden by Christopher Lloyd. Collins
Foliage Plants by Christopher Lloyd. Collins
Clematis by Christopher Lloyd. Collins
The Dictionary of Garden Plants by Hay & Singe. Ebury/RHS
The Dictionary of Shrubs by S. Millar Goult. Ebury/RHS
The Rose by Jack Harkness. Macmillan
Roses by Jack Harkness. Dent
Hilliers' Manual of Trees and Shrubs. Hilliers
Plants for Ground Cover by G. Stuart Thomas. Dent
Climbing Roses Old and New by G. Stuart Thomas. Dent
Old Shrub Roses by G. Stuart Thomas. Dent
Perennial Garden Plants by G. Stuart Thomas. Dent
The Dry Garden by Beth Chatto. Dent
The New Small Garden by C. E. Lucas Phillips. Collins
The International Book of Trees by Hugh Johnson. Mitchell Beazley
The Principles of Gardening by Hugh Johnson. Mitchell Beazley
Vita Sackville-West's Garden Book. Michael Joseph
Guide to the Gardens of Britain & Europe. Granada
Gardens of the National Trust by G. Stuart Thomas. Weidenfeld
Simple Propagation by Noel J. Prockter. Faber
The Fruit Garden Displayed by Royal Horticultural Society. RHS
The Vegetable Garden Displayed by Royal Horticultural Society. RHS
RHS Handbooks on many subjects are most useful.

APPENDIX VI

Addresses of some suppliers

Allwood Bros, Clayton Nursery, Hassocks, W. Sussex. *Carnations and pinks.*
Ashfield Herb Nursery, Hinstock, Market Drayton, Salop. *Herbs.*
David Austin, Bowling Green Lane, Albrighton, Wolverhampton. *Roses, especially old-fashioned.*
Avon Bulbs, Bathford, Bath. *Miniature and uncommon bulbs.*

Peter Beales, Intwood Nurseries, Swardeston, Norwich. *Specialist in old-fashioned roses.*
Blackmore and Langdon, Pensford Nursery, Bristol. *Delphiniums and begonias.*
Bressingham Gardens, Diss, Norfolk. *Herbaceous and conifers.*
Broadleigh Gardens, Barr House, Bishops Hill, Taunton, Somerset. *Small bulbs.*
Butcher Ltd, Shirley, Croydon, Surrey. *Seeds.*

Cants, The Old Rose Gardens, Stanway, Colchester, Essex. *Roses.*
Thomas Carlisle, Carlisle's Corner, Twyford, Reading, Berks. *Herbaceous, alpine.*
Richard Cawthorne, 3 Ivor Grove, New Eltham, London S.E.9. *Viola specialist.*
Beth Chatto, White Barn House, Elmstead Market, Nr. Colchester, Essex. *Unusual plants.*
Cockers Roses, Whitemyres, Langstracht, Aberdeen. *Roses.*
County Park Nurseries, Essex Gardens, Hornchurch, Essex. *New Zealand plants, hebes.*

de Jagers, Marden, Kent. *Excellent bulbs, lily specialists.*
Denbigh Heather Nurseries. All Saints' Road, Creeting St Mary, Ipswich.
Dickson Nurseries, Newtownards, Co. Down, N. Ireland. *Roses.*
Dobies Seeds, Upper Dee Mills, Llangollen, Clwyd. *Good seed catalogue.*

Fibrex Nurseries, Harvey Rd, Evesham, Worcs. *Geraniums, pelargoniums.*
Fisk's Clematis Nursery, Westleton, Nr Saxmundham, Suffolk. *Clematis.*
Fryers Nursery, Knutsford, Cheshire. *Roses.*

Gardener's Catalogue, P.O. Box 54, Burton Latimer, Northants. *Interesting range of tools and accessories at good prices.*
Great Dixter Nurseries, Northiam, Sussex. *Christopher Lloyd's clematis and other plants.*
Gregory's Roses, Toton Lane, Stapleford, Nottingham. *General catalogue with biggest range of miniatures.*

L. Hall, Broadway Nurseries, High Heath, Pensall, Walsall. *Chrysanthemums.*
Harkness Roses, Cambridge Rd, Hitchin, Herts. *Roses.*
Highfield Nurseries, Whitminster, Glos. *Fruit and general*
Highland's Water Garden, Soulsbridge Lane, Chorley Wood, Herts. *Everything for the pond.*
Hilliers' Nurseries, Winchester, Hants. *Largest selection of trees and shrubs. Their manual of trees and shrubs is essential.*
V. H. Humphrey, 8 Howbeck Rd, Arnold, Nottingham. *Irises.*
Hydon Nurseries, Clock Basin Lane, Hydon Heath, Godalming, Surrey. *Rhododendrons, azaleas, camellias.*

W. Ingwersen, Birch Farm Nursery, Gravetye, E. Grinstead, W. Sussex. *Marvellous collection of rock plants and miniature bulbs.*

Jefferson Brown, Waylite, Martley, Worcester. *Daffodils and grape vines.*

Kelways, Langport, Somerset. *Many bulbs and herbaceous. Famous for irises and peonies.*
The Knoll Gardens, Stapehill Rd, Stapehill, Wimborne, Dorset. *Rare shrubs.*

E. B. LeGrise, North Walsham, Norfolk. *Unusual roses.*
C. S. Lockyer, 70 Henfield Rd, Coalpit Heath, Bristol. *Fuchsias.*

Marshalls Seeds, Wisbech, Cambridge. *Good smallish seed catalogue.*
John Mattock, Nuneham Courtney, Oxford. *Roses*
Meilland Star Roses, 464 Goff's Lane, Goff's Oak, Waltham Cross, Herts. *Roses.*
Ken Muir, Honeypot Farm, Weeley Heath, Clacton, Essex. *Soft fruit.*

Norton Hall Nurseries, 115 Kynaston Rd, Panfield, Braintree, Essex. *Day lilies and irises.*
Notcutts, Woodbridge, Suffolk. *Large excellent selection of trees, shrubs and plants.*

Pennell and Sons, Princess St, Lincoln. *Clematis.*

Rampart's Nurseries, Baker's Lane, Braiswick, Colchester. *Silver-leaved plants.*
Robinsons, Knockholt, Sevenoaks, Kent. *Heathers and conifers*
R. V. Roger, The Nurseries, Pickering, Yorks. *Roses and general.*
L. R. Russel, Richmond Nurseries, Windlesham, Surrey. *Trees and shrubs, herbaceous.*

Scotts Nurseries, Merriott, Somerset. *Large general trees, shrubs and herbaceous.*
Sherrads, Snelsmore Rd, Donnington, Newbury, Berks. *Interesting trees, shrubs and roses.*
Mrs J. Abel Smith, Orchard House, Letty Green, Nr Hertford. *Unusual daffodils.*
South Down Nurseries, Southgate St, Redruth, Cornwall. *Interesting herbaceous plants and shrubs.*
Spalding Bulb Co., Horseshoe Rd, Spalding, Lincs. *Bulbs.*
Stapeley Water Gardens, Stapeley, Nantwich, Cheshire. *Everything for your pond.*
Sunningdale Nurseries, Windlesham, Surrey. *Wide choice, general.*
Suttons Seeds, Hele Rd, Torquay, Devon. *Large selection, good seeds.*

Thompson and Morgan, Dept PRGN, London Rd, Ipswich, Suffolk. *Unusual seeds.*

Thorpe's Nurseries, 257 Finchampstead Rd, Wokingham, Berks. *Geraniums and pelargoniums.*

James Trehane, Stapehill Rd, Hampreston, Wimborne, Dorset. *Camellias.*

Tumblers Bottom Herb Farm, Kilmersdon, Radstock, Somerset. *Large herb selection.*

Unwins Seeds, Histon, Cambridge. *Good seeds, large sweet pea collection.*

Van Tubergen, Willow Bank Wharf, Ranelagh Gardens, London SW6. *Dutch bulbs.*

Webbs, Long Acre Gardens, Bagstone, Wickwar, Wooton under Edge, Glos. *Geraniums and pelargoniums.*

Wells and Winter, Mereworth, Maidstone, Kent. *Herb specialists.*

Alan Wren, Beechview Nursery, Avery Lane, Waltham Abbey, Essex. *Chrysanthemums.*

Wheatcroft Roses, Edwalton, Nottingham. *Roses.*

APPENDIX VII

Some useful addresses

ABC Publications, 40 Bowling Green Lane, London EC1. Publish annually *Historic Houses, Castles and Gardens open to the Public.*

The Alpine Gardens Society, Lye End Link, St Johns, Woking, Surrey.

The Electricity Council, 30 Millbank, London SW1.

Gardeners' Sunday, White Witches, Claygate Road, Dorking, Surrey. Publish *Gardens to Visit,* covering private gardens.

The Garden History Society, 11 St Paul's Road East, Dorking, Surrey.

The Hardy Plant Society, 10 St Barnabas Road, Emmer Green, Caversham, Berks.

The Henry Doubleday Research Association, Convent Lane, Bocking, Braintree, Essex.

The Herb Society, 34 Boscobel Place, London SW1.

The National Gardens Scheme, 57 Lower Belgrave Street, London SW1.

The National Vegetable Society, 29 Revidge Road, Blackburn, Lancs.

The Orchid Society, 28 Felday Road, Lewisham, London SE13.

The Royal Horticultural Society, Vincent Square, London SW1.

The Royal National Rose Society, Bone Hill, Chiswell Green Lane, St Albans, Herts.

The Soil Association, Walnut Tree Manor, Houghley, Stowmarket, Suffolk. Publish booklets on compost, soil improvement etc.

The Tradescant Trust, 7 Little Boltons, London SW10.

INDEX

Acanthus mollis latifolius, 57
acer (maple), 119–20
  A. albomarginatum, 120
  A. japonicum, 88, 120
  A. negundo, 120
  A. palmatum, 120
  A. saccharinum, 120
achillea, 85
acidanthera, 148
aconite, 41
adiantum (maidenhair fern),
  154
agapanthus, 66, 108, 148, 149
alchemilla, 41, 61, 62, 67, 83,
  86
allium, 149
  A. albopilosum, 149
  A. giganteum, 149
  A moly luteum, 150
  A. neapolitanum, 150
allotment, 72–3
alpines, 11–12
alstroemeria, 148, 150
alyssum, 11, 12, 50, 87, 104,
  161
amaryllis, 148
  A. belladonna, 14, 150
Androsace carnea, 11
anemone, 66, 89, 114
  A. blanda, 19
annuals, 27–8, 112
Anthemis cupaniana, 67
  A. nobilis (camomile), 69
antirrhinum (snapdragon),
  39, 50, 86, 87, 104, 159,
  161
Aponogeton distachyus
  (water hawthorn), 163
apple, 109, 110–12, 147
aquilegia (columbine), 14, 42,
  68, 86, 132
arabis, 11, 12
Armeria caespitosa, 11
artemisia, 8, 57, 83
  A. arborescens, 57
artichoke, globe, 8–9, 83, 85
arum lily, 83
astilbe, 42
aubergine, 22, 35
aubrieta, 11, 12
aucuba, 89
avocado, 140, 141
azalea, 31–2, 138–9

Barnsley House, 61, 62
basement garden, 102–4

basil, 3, 4, 47, 49, 89
bay tree, 4, 94, 136
beans, 20
  broad, 22, 151
  French, 22
  runner, 8, 22, 52, 87
  seed, 132–3
  sprouting, 49
bedding plants, 38
Bedgbury Pinetum, 119
beech, 121
beetroot, 9, 20, 22, 48, 151
begonia, 52, 126, 148, 149,
  159
Berberis vulgaris
  Atropurpurea, 83, 84
bergenia, 5, 56, 83, 107
  B. schmidtii, 5
birch (betula), 121, 123
  B. pendula, 123–4
blackberry, 109
blackcurrant, 109, 147
bluebell, 113
bonemeal, *see* fertilizer
Borde Hill, 67
bougainvillea, 80
boysenberry, 109, 110
broccoli, 20, 22, 48, 151
Brookes, John, 93
Brussels sprouts, 20, 22, 48,
  151
buddleia, 71, 101
  B. davidii Harlequin, 101
bulbs, 112
  indoor, 95–7
  spring, 114–15
  summer, 148–51
busy lizzie (impatiens), 52,
  161

cabbage, 20, 22, 151
  Chinese, 22, 52
  Savoy, 73
  winter, 73
calendula, *see* marigold
camellia, 23–4, 40–41
  C. japonica, 41
  C. williamsii, 41
camomile lawn, 69
campanula, 11, 12, 62, 68
  C. poscharskyana, 68
candytuft, 27, 68
Canterbury bell, 132
carrot, 20, 22, 36, 48, 73, 151
caryopteris, 108
  C. clandonensis, 108

catalpa, 121
catananche, 85
cauliflower, 20, 22
Cawthorne, Richard, 97, 98, 99
ceanothus, 155, 165
celeriac, 22
celery, 20, 22
chaenomeles (Japanese
  quince), 17, 41, 166
  C. japonica, 18
  C. speciosa, 17–18
chamaecyparis, 139
  Minima Aurea, 140
chamaedorea, 152
  C. elegans, 153
chard, 9
Chatto, Beth, 56–57
cherry, *see* Prunus
chicory, 22, 48
chionodoxa, 89, 114
chives, 3, 4, 35, 47, 49, 89
Choisya ternata, 14, 40, 66,
  83, 104
chrysanthemum, 12–13, 83
cineraria, 39
Cissus antarctica (kangaroo
  vine), 152–3
cistus (rock rose), 57, 71
citrus fruit, 141
clematis, 37, 87, 103, 155–6,
  164, 165
  C. alpina, 62, 156
  C. armandii, 156
  C. balearica, 66
  C. henryi, 66, 90, 156
  C. jackmanii, 90, 103, 155,
    156, 166
  C. montana, 90, 103, 156,
    166, 167
  C. orientalis, 156
  C. vitalba, 155
  C. viticella, 155
climbing plants, 164–7;
  see also clematis,
  honeysuckle *etc.*
club root, 48
Cobaea scandens, 90, 161, 167
Cocker, Alex, 77
codiaeum (croton), 154
colchicum, 108
  C. autumnale, 108
compost, 115, 127–8, 167–8
Convolvulus cneorum, 67
cordyline, 62
coriander, 4
cornflower, 14, 27

cornus,
  C. *alba*, 101
  C. *kousa chinensis*, 122
cotoneaster,
  C. *frigidus*, 107
  C. *horizontalis*, 101, 107
courgette (zucchini), 9, 20,
  22, 47, 48, 133
crocus, 5, 97, 104, 108
cucumber, 20, 22, 33, 35, 47, 48
  seed, 132, 161
Culpeper Complete Herbal, 4
cuttings, 69–71
  chrysanthemum, 13
  dahlia, 13
  geranium, 71–2
  viola, 98
cyclamen, 137–8
cypress, 121
  C. *leylandii*, 121
  C. *sempervirens*, 122

daffodil, 89, 104, 113, 114;
  see also narcissus
dahlia, 12–13, 37, 126, 148,
  149, 164
daphne,
  D. *mezereum*, 145
  D. *odora*, 89, 145
day lily (hemerocallis), 14,
  42, 132
delphinium, 14, 61, 62, 65, 132
design, garden, 93–5
deutzia, 71
  D. *setchuenensis*, 66
dianthus, 12
  D. *alpinus*, 11
diervilla, *see* weigela
digging, 115–16
D'Ombrain, Honeywood, 63
Douglas, David, 119
dried flowers, 85–6
dry places, plants for, 56–7

echinops (globe thistle), 85
  E. *humilis* Taplow Blue,
  108
  E. *ritro*, 108
edelweiss, 12
elaeagnus, 71, 89, 100, 136
  E. *pungens* Maculata, 62,
  137, 146
endive, 48
Eryngium maritimum, 85
Eucalyptus gunnii, 123
euonymus, 71, 89
  E. *fortunei*, 62, 70, 100
  E. *japonica* Ovatus
  Aureus, 100

euphorbia (spurge), 57, 83, 84
  E. *characias*, 6, 57
  E. *polychroma*, 57

Fatsia japonica, 146
fennel, 3, 4, 22
fertilizer,
  bonemeal, 36, 104
  Growmore, 36, 48
  lawn, 26
  Phostrogen, 48, 51, 89
feverfew, 61
Ficus benjamina, 152, 153
flower arranging, 82–5
  Christmas, 136–7
forget-me-not, 31, 113
forsythia, 17
  F. *suspensa*, 146
foxglove (digitalis), 42, 68,
  132
fruit, 109–12
  family tree, 112
  pruning, 147–8
  spraying, 147
furniture, garden, 37–8
fuchsia, 8, 87, 126

Gambier, Lord, 98
Garrya elliptica, 137, 146,
  166
gentian, 11, 12
geranium (pelargonium), 11,
  38, 67, 71, 89, 103, 113
  cuttings, 71–72
  hanging baskets, 37, 50, 51
  overwintering, 33, 125–6
  from seed, 132, 159, 160
  window box, 39, 124
Geranium endressii, 68
Ginkgo bibola, 122
gladiolus, 148, 149, 150
Gleditschia triacanthos, 123
godetia, 27
gooseberry, 109, 110, 147
grape hyacinth (muscari),
  19, 97
grass, ornamental, 85
greenhouse, 32–4, 94, 159, 161
gro-bag, 9, 35
ground cover, 56–7, 66–7,
  174
gypsophila, 66

Hamamelis mollis, 146
hanging basket, 50–51, 103, 153
Harkness, Jack, 63
heather, 85, 139–40
  Calluna vulgaris, 140

Erica carnea, 140
hebe, 14, 56, 71, 84, 104,
  168–9
  H x *andersonii*, 168
  H. Bowles' Hybrid, 168, 169
  H x *franciscana*
  Variegata, 101, 169
  H. *macrantha*, 169
  H. Pagei, 67, 125, 139, 168,
  169
  H. *rakaiensis*, 139
helianthemum (rock rose),
  11, 12, 56, 68
helichrysum (straw flower),
  27, 85
  H. *petiolatum*, 39, 50
hellebore, 42, 83
  H. *corsicus*, 5, 42
  H. *niger*, 5, 42, 145
  H. *orientalis*, 5, 42
Helxine soleirolii (mind-
  your-own-business), 154
herbs, 3–4, 47, 94
herbaceous plants, 13–14
Hidcote, 61, 62
Hills, Lawrence, 86
Hole, Reynolds, 63
holly (ilex), 62, 101, 134–5,
  136
  I. *altaclarensis*, 135
  I. *aquifolium*, 134–5, 136
hollyhock, 132
honesty (lunaria), 85
honeysucke (lonicera), 37,
  41, 66, 68, 87, 164, 165
  L. x *americana*, 167
  L. *japonica* Halliana, 90, 103
  L. *nitida* Baggesen's Gold,
  62
hop, 62
hosta, 14, 41, 62, 83, 86
  H. *crispula*, 41, 68
  H. *decorata*, 68
  H. *fortunei*, 41, 68
  H. *plantaginea*, 41
  H. *sieboldiana*, 41, 68
house-plants, 152–4
Howea forsteriana
  (paradise palm), 153
hyacinth, 95–6
hydrangea, 41, 71, 85, 107
  H. *petiolaris*, 41, 66, 165
hydroponics, 154
hypericum,
  H. *calycinum*, 67
  H. *patulum* Hidcote, 62

iberis, 12
Ingwersen, Will, 11

insecticide, 55
iris, 41, 66, 150–51, 161, 163
  I. foetidissima, 57, 150
  I. laevigata, 163
  I. reticulata, 5, 97
  I. unguicularis, 5, 150
ivy (hedera), 67, 83, 101,
  103, 104, 134, 136, 165,
  166
  H. canariensis Gloire de
    Marengo, 135
  H. colchica dentata
    Variegata, 135
  H. helix, 135, 152
  H. helix Goldheart, 89,
    135, 136
ixia (corn lily), 149

jasmine, 66
  J. officinale, 90
Jekyll, Gertrude, 5, 14
Johnson, Lawrence, 61
juniper, 139
  J. virginiana Skyrocket, 89

kale, 9, 20, 22
kerria, 165

laburnum, 31, 62, 165
lamium, 56, 67
larkspur, 14, 27
lavatera (mallow), 27, 132
  161
lavender (lavandula), 3, 4, 8,
  77, 84
  L. spica, 137
  L. spica Hidcote, 125
lawn, 24–6
leek, 20, 22, 87
lettuce, 9, 20, 22, 35, 47, 52,
  73
  seed, 87, 132, 161
lilac (syringa), 31, 126–7
  S. vulgaris, 126
lily, 14, 62, 133–4, 148, 149,
  159, 155
  L. auratum, 133, 134
  L. canadense, 133
  L. henryi, 42, 133
  L. martagon, 42, 133
  L. monadelphum, 133
  L. pardalinum, 133
  L. regale, 66, 133, 134
  L. speciosum, 133
lime, 121
limnanthes (poached egg
  flower), 27
Limonium sinuatum (sea
  lavender), 85

lobelia, 50, 52, 87, 104, 132,
  161
loganberry, 109
lovage, 3
love-in-a-mist (nigella), 14,
  27, 85
lupin, 14, 132

Macqueen, Sheila, 83
mahonia, 89
  M. aquifolium, 40, 146
  M x Charity, 8, 145
  M. japonica, 145
Mallin, Hester, 87, 89
malus (crab apple), 107–8
manure, 115, 167
maple, see acer
marigold (calendula,
  tagetes), 27, 39, 50, 159
  French, 104, 161
marjoram, 4, 49
marrow, 9, 52, 133
melon, 22
Michaelmas daisy, 14, 108
mint, 3, 49, 89
morning glory (ipomoea),
  161, 167
mulberry, 109
mustard and cress, 49

narcissus, 5, 18–19, 114;
  see also daffodil
  indoors, 95–6
  N. canaliculatus, 114
  N. cyclamineus, 114
  N. lobularis, 114
nasturtium, 27–8
Nerine bowdenii, 14
nicotiana (tobacco plant),
  14, 39, 66, 87, 104, 108,
  113, 132, 161
nitrogen, 36, 168
Nymans, 61

office, vegetables in, 48–9
oleander, 69, 80, 94, 125
onion, 20, 22, 55, 87, 151
origano, 62

pansy, 52, 86, 97, 98, 99, 132,
  161
parsley, 4, 47, 89
parsnip, 20, 22, 36, 151
passion flower, 165
paving, 94
pea, 20, 21, 22
peach, 147
pear, 109, 110–12, 147;
  see also pyrus

peat, 116
pelargonium, see geranium
peony, 14, 45–6, 62
  P. mlokosewitschii, 46
  P. suffruticosa, 46
peperomia (desert privet),
  154
pepper, green, 9, 22, 33, 35,
  47, 49, 161
pergola, 37, 94
periwinckle (vinca), 67, 101,
  146
pests, garden, 55
petunia, 38, 39, 52, 86, 87,
  89, 103, 104
  hanging basket, 50
  seed, 132, 159, 160
philodendron,
  P. lacineatum, 153
  P. scandens (sweetheart
    vine), 153
phlox, 14
  P. drummondii, 161
phosphorus, 36, 168
Physalis franchetti, 85
Phytolacca americana, 83
pineapple, 140–41
pink, 14, 68, 87
pips, plants from, 140–41
pittosporum, 101
  P. tenuifolium, 102
planting, fruit, 109–12
plum, 110, 111, 147
poinsettia (Euphorbia
  pulcherrima), 138
pollination, fruit-tree, 111
polyanthus, 112, 113
polygonatum (Solomon's
  seal), 41
polygonum (Russian vine),
  90, 167
pool, garden, 161–3
poplar, 121
poppy, 84, 85
potash, 36
potato, 19, 20, 21, 47, 73,
  163–4
potentilla, 11
primrose, 5, 19, 113
primula, 41
  P. altaica, 19
  P. bulleyana, 42
  P. florindae, 42
  P. japonica, 42
  P. vulgaris, see primrose
Prockter, Noel, 70
pruning,
  fruit, 147–8
  roses, 6–8

prunus (cherry), 17, 147
 P. *lauroceras*, 4
 P. *padus* Grandiflora, 17
 P. *subhirtella*, 17
pyracantha, 41, 107, 164, 165
 P *atalantioides*, 107
 P. *coccinea*, 101
pyrus,
 P. *nivalis*, 123
 P *salicifolia* Pendula, 123

quince, flowering, *see*
 chaenomeles

radish, 20, 22, 73
raspberry, 89, 109, 110, 147
redcurrant, 89, 109, 110, 147
rhododendron, 31, 32
Rhoicissus rhomboidea
 (grape ivy), 152, 153
Rhus typhina, 120
Robinia pseudoacacia, 123
rock garden, 10–12
rock rose, *see* cistus,
 helianthemum
rooftop gardening, 51–2,
 87–90
rose, 37, 62–5, 68, 77–8, 155
 Bourbon, 64
 climbing, 90, 165, 166
 floribunda, 77, 78
 hybrid musk, 64–5
 hybrid tea, 77
 miniature, 52–4
 polyantha, 65
 pruning, 6–8
 rambling, 65, 90
 R. *rubrifolia*, 64
 R. *rugosa*, 64
 for shade, 41, 103
 shrub, 107
 standard, 65
rosemary, 3, 4, 47, 104, 125
Roserie de l'Hay-les-Roses,
 65, 166
Royal National Rose Society,
 7, 52, 63
rue, 4, 57, 62, 104

Sackville-West, Vita, 61, 123
sage, 4, 47, 62, 89, 104
salsify, 22
salvia, 87
Sambucus nigra
 Aureomarginata, 83
santolina (cotton lavender),
 4, 57, 77, 125
 S. *incana* Nana, 125
savory, 3, 4, 49

saxifrage, 11, 12
scabious, 27
scilla, 19, 46, 89, 104
sea lavender, *see* limonium
sedum (iceplant), 57, 83, 108
 S. *maximum*
 Atropurpureum, 108
seed,
 choosing, 131–3
 saving, 86–7
 sowing, 159–61
 testing, 151
senecio, 57
 S. *cineraria*, 50
 S. *greyi*, 8, 39, 70, 84, 104,
 125
shade, plants for, 40–42, 171
shallot, 151
Sissinghurst, 61, 69, 71
Skimmia japonica, 41, 137
snapdragon, *see* antirrhinum
snowdrop, 5, 89, 95, 97, 104
soil, 56, 115–16
 feeding, 167–8
Soil Association, 54, 55
sorbus (mountain ash),
 S. *aucuparia*, 107
 S. *hupehensis*, 107
sorrel, 3, 4, 47
sowing,
 lawn, 25
 vegetable seed, 20–22
spinach, 22, 48, 73, 87
spiraea, 71
spraying, fruit trees, 147–8
Spry, Constance, 82
squash, 22
stachys, 57, 67
stephanotis, 35
strawberry, 80–82, 89
sunflower, 27
swede, 20
sweetcorn, 52
sweet pea, 27, 66, 86, 87, 90,
 99–100, 109, 131, 161, 165,
 167
syngonium (goose foot), 154

tagetes, *see* marigold
tarragon, 4, 47
taxus (yew),
 T. *baccata* Fastigiata, 122
terrarium, 154
thyme, 3, 4, 47, 89
 lawn, 68–9
tobacco plant, *see* nicotiana
tomato, 9–10, 20, 22, 33, 37,
 47, 48, 49, 52
 seed, 87, 161

tools, 24
tradescantia (wandering jew),
 152, 153, 154
trees, 119–20
 evergreen, 121–3
 planting, 120–21
 silver, 123–4
tubs,
 camellias, 24
 plants for, 172–3
 trees and shrubs for, 173–4
tulip, 89, 114
 T. *fosteriana*, 114
 T. *greigii*, 115
 T. *kaufmanniana*, 114
 T. *tarda*, 115

valerian, 132
variegated shrubs, 100–102
vegetables, 47–8
 decorative, 8–9
 gro-bags, 35
 office grown, 48–9
 seeds, 132–3
 spring sowing, 19–22
 unusual, 22
verbascum, 61, 65, 132
veronica, 12
Verey, Rosemary, 61
viburnum,
 V. *davidii*, 41
 V. *tinus*, 8, 84
vinca, *see* periwinkle
vine, 28, 104
viola, 41, 62, 97–9, 132
 V. *cornuta*, 97, 98
Virginia creeper, 104, 165
viscaria, 27

wallflower, 31, 104, 113, 124, 132
water lily (nymphaea), 161, 162
 N. Froebelii, 162
 N. x *marliacea*
 Chromatella, 162
watering, 79–80
weeds, value of, 54–5
Weigela florida Variegata,
 62, 84, 101
Westonbirt Arboretum, 119
window box, 38–40, 88, 104
 plants for, 172–3
 winter, 124–5
winter garden, 145–7
wisteria, 31, 165
 W. *sinensis* Alba, 66

yew, *see* taxus
yucca, 57
 Y. *gloriosa*, 62